I0520616

Profound Pondering

By Eyan Bryant

Vol.1

Copyright ©2025 Profound Pondering LLC

All Rights Reserved

This book serves as a work of creative philosophy and internal reflection. No part of this
publication may be reproduced, distributed, or transmitted in any form or by any means
without prior written authorization of the publisher, except in the case of brief cited
quotations embodied in review or personal study.

Written by Eyan Bryant

Published by:

Profound Pondering LLC

P.O. Box 10010

Columbus, OH 43201-3501

www.Profoundpondering.com

ISBN: 979-8-9992395-0-1

First edition, 2025

Printed in the United States of America

Profound Pondering

To my Grandmother

For all of your love and support

And to my brother

For giving me an opportunity to see how I needed to change

TABLE OF CONTENTS

Expression

Perspective

Wholeness

FOREWORD

Good day,

Allow this to serve as a gentle reminder that all we can ever be is people, and no one person is an island alone. When we explore topics such as mental health, mindfulness, spirituality, etc., we must recognize that we can only learn if we are willing to listen. In my life so far, I have endeavored and labored with many of the ideas presented within this book. I share this with you all in the hope that you do not need to spend so much time in your mind, when the world is where you are. In finding our place in the world, we're really just giving ourselves the space we already take up. Many of the things we reach for would already be in our possession if we retracted our hands. In the same light, the information I share with this is not new in the slightest, nor is it inherent to any individual person. The knowledge of the world belongs to those who inhabit it and if we are to truly be people, then it must be shared. All we are ever doing is sharing a perspective, so we must learn to share with love. If we choose not to share, we are really only taking from ourselves. When we point at the world, it points back, for you are part of what you point at. The same idea goes for people and circumstances, as labels and connotations are felt by the ones who accept and place them. So, this exploration is for those who want to see a part of the perspective, and one that has served to benefit many so far. Some individuals may be coming from their interactions with the YouTube channel Profound Pondering, and some may just be here by chance. Regardless of which, thank you for being here and thank you for being you. As for the content of this book, it should all be interpreted as one would free verse/word poetry. And while there are poems included, the excerpts are in no concrete order. There was much intentionality in terms of what section each writing belongs to; however, when it comes to the content itself, they differ at least in one way.

Profound Pondering is an interpretation of self-awareness that allows it to serve as a benefit, rather than a detriment. Many of us find that when we become aware of ourselves, many negative things begin to plague our thoughts. And via said thoughts, our perceptions and actions fall short of what we genuinely desire for ourselves. To input any type of positivity into one's mind is adding another stone to the path you walk. Not to say it makes the path, but to say that it makes it easier to navigate. Each path we walk is only as free as we allow it to be, and our direction is chosen for us if we do not choose for ourselves. The point I find is to make a choice, not in what direction to go, but in which person to be. For if we get to know the self, then the path we walk will show itself to us, as we show ourselves to the path.

Profound Pondering

The first relationship that any of us have to anything, starts with the one we have with ourselves. There is no situation of the mind that is not colored with our biases. For if it were not biased, then it would cease to be a situation, and we might regard it as a thought. If we can recognize that our experience is determined by what we choose ourselves to be. Then we will begin to make decisions that have us in mind. Who we are may at times not seem like something that we have a say in. Our initial circumstances, our parents, our education, all at first are made for us. However, once we become aware of this, we have some influence on what is yet to be. Awareness is one of the greatest weapons that a person can have at their disposal. The problem that many people face with this awareness is not using it for their own benefit. We pilot our lives as if we have infinite time to do as we please yet look at it as if there is none left. When we depend on time to guide us we are often confined by it. In thinking about ourselves within the scale of time we often displace our growth with its idea. Change is always something that occurs in the future rather than the present from this viewpoint. And to mitigate such an idea, we must accept that both the future and past are nonexistent. The present is the only place where a future can be built, so the intention should not be on leaving the past, but creating the future.

What this novel hopes to achieve is not much of an achievement at all. When we come to realize that what we search for is only lost in our search, we are often left at the same place we started. This in no way of the word is a negative thing, as we all have moments that define us. And all moments are in the present.

Section One:

FOUNDATIONS

Who am I? What should I be doing? How should I feel?

Many of these questions stem from our lack of address of what is currently here. Our center has to be where we are, otherwise, we will never be. In placing foundation within the self, the self becomes the foundation.

FOUNDATIONS

Anything can be everything

When we begin to address what we do, we must first address the one that is doing it. One of life's most important lessons is to learn how to enjoy being who you are, free from the influence of others' perceptions. What we do, whether we like it or not, is dictated by how we feel about ourselves. If we don't know ourselves enough to know what we genuinely want, we find ourselves lost in what we are told to desire. *The meaning contained within life is given by those who live it*, and we are not permitted entry into the world until we stop living in our minds.

Many parts of life have the ability to pollute an individual, as "a man must be a sea to receive pollution and not become polluted himself"[1] - Friedrich Nietzsche. Nietzsche was a German philosopher who spoke deeply about the conditioning of man. This with direct reference to how we are impacted by our own perceptions, of both who we are and our own depth. To be a "sea" from this viewpoint is in simple terms, to get out of your own way. And this quote radiates the importance of allowing a broad perspective of who you are. *It's to let yourself go and begin to swim, without worry of getting wet.* We often only have the capacity that we grant ourselves, first in mind. So, the stress of life isn't to not encounter pollution, rather to expand your definition until no amount of negativity will pollute the waters of your identity.

Profound Pondering

Within the world we inhabit, there exists a darkness which can only exist in reference to light. And I think we must realize that within each of us, both find their dwelling. Interaction with such entities of positivity and negativity is only possible if we are able to interact with ourselves. It can be said that as long as the light is coming from you, no shadows will be cast. We must learn to give ourselves the spoils of our own harvests. Our validation, our love, our understanding, are not things that we must receive from the world around us. Rather, things we must give to ourselves.

When we don't recognize that the self is expressed in all that we do, we can find ourselves lost in search for what is right in front of us. *If being yourself is all you ever can do, what good would come from stressing the self to fit some image, other than the one that already exists?* We don't need to have a perfect image, we just need to be willing to work on the art that is the self. *We are both sculpture and sculptor all at once, aiming to never be finished, yet in the constant production of something beautiful.* What we are able to provide for ourselves is often precisely what we need to begin the work. The love you have for anything can be representative of the love you have for everything. However, if we never begin to love who we are, we will find subtle difficulty in loving the world *we* inhabit . For if we base the love we have for the world in the lack we have in ourselves, we will love in reference to what we lack, instead of what we possess. *And the aim isn't to have possessions to love, rather to love yourself as you would a possession.*

There must come a point where we take some responsibility in seeing the world from our point of view. This said, it's important to evaluate how it is you prescribe value, to what it is that you do and see. Many times, in life, we undermine ourselves in an effort to exist in a relative comfort of ideas. We like to think about our peace in reference to what's outside of us, rather than what's inside. Peace is not found, it's created out of our willingness to see who we are, and learning to navigate the patterns of our own understanding. When it comes to our desires, we should realize that there is no limit to what we can find, especially in regard to what we contain within. We can only get as much as we give, and in many cases, we put only part of who we are into what we do. For this reason, we are unable to truly dictate what parts of ourselves can be brought about by our actions. To say anything can be everything is to say that it's important to be present enough to realize what serves you. Any one thing or event can either be the source of our bliss or our despair, depending on how we allow our perspective to shift into it. I find that putting yourself fully into situations allows you to get yourself fully out of them. The more we realize that we aren't the situations we encounter, the more apt we will be to see things for what they are. The longer we place our value in outcomes, the longer our value will be separate from us. Ultimately, your worth is what you carry with you, not something that is presented in front of you.

FOUNDATIONS

Sonder

The realization that everyone lives their own complex life. All of us encounter problems both physically and mentally. However, even with the realization that everyone has a life of their own, we still neglect the shared space that is the world. Our preoccupation with our viewpoint often causes us to forget that we have many ways of looking at individual issues. It is when we don't acknowledge other possibilities that they do not exist.

Throughout the time of man our own desires have plagued our consciousness. The nature of man we currently exemplify is that of selfishness. In most ways the pursuit of material is only a temporary fix to satiate how we feel about ourselves. *We find our own value in things we give value to, for if we had none to give, then we would have none to receive.* It is because we have value that we are able to see it in the world around us. We tend to impart value from ourselves and seek said value in things that are deemed "valuable".

In past times I've thought of the necessity for ego, however that's only in a sense of self-identity, and not the egotistical expression of our disposition. To what extent is our own self-identity the cause for our selfish behavior?

If we never discovered or found better yet realized individuality, then many of the world's surface issues would cease. We keep only ourselves in mind while plotting out goals. Being an individual myself, I don't see much wrong with that in a sense of each person's personal journey. Why should my desires be governed or halted by people other than myself?

Even our individual commitment to ourselves can only exist in a balanced dosage. That is to say that human ills must have limits and or points where desire of the individual is no longer valid. This point would have to be when how a desire is pursued causes direct harm to others.

I think in our minds we can never experience what others do. To the same standard understanding, this can only occur if both sides are willing to share in each other's perspectives. We know that everyone has their own complex life but we fail to realize what makes them special.

We all are a path, and some of us are fortunate enough to realize we can create our own. We struggle, prevail, hope and despair all in the same life. It's this condensed existence that allows people to be themselves exploring all angles of their being.

FOUNDATIONS

Being alone

Among all the things that we humans do, being alone has one of the most negative connotations. We spend our entire lives being told that in order to be complete,

you have to have people around. Like when we were young and parents might say something along the lines of, "One day you'll have a beautiful wife and kids". Not that the push for connection is something that is wrong, rather we can't truly, until we connect with ourselves.

Always having something to lean back onto is a blessing many don't possess. However, could it be said that this is a good thing? Throughout our lives we are constantly fermenting an idea of self, primarily through our interactions with the external world. Friends and experiences alike are an uncomplicated way to determine a simple idea of who we are. The main issue is that our internal values from this view are dependent on the perspective of others. Since people are close and you trust them, you believe what they say and attach it to yourself, of course some props should be used to assist the house. However, a house is truly complete only if it can stand without its props. The issue with leaning on the judgment of friends and family is that when they're gone or aren't as close to you in some way, you take the blame. This image that you have developed from the perspective of others is no more and you begin to collapse. Growing up with people to create an identity creates comfort and dangerously at that.

You think that you for the most part have it figured out. However, when the support or attention leaves, so does the comfort you once felt. This is when people begin to question how genuine they are as people and ask the question, "To what extent is who I am in an external sense genuine?". The people who rely and are surrounded by those who dictate identity suffer from not being able to dictate it themselves.

It can be said however that the first prescribed identity does undergo change. We all change in order to adapt and to grow. What I realize is we at times do not know whether the change was done for us or to maintain the image created by others.

Some of the parts of our personality that were altered by the thoughts of others are what lead to issues in the now. This can also be said about the repetitive thoughts we may have about ourselves. We discard the parts of ourselves that have negative connotations in order to change for society and who we are around. This is why I feel people are always feeling as if something is missing. However, that missing part is the "you" that you have left behind. The point should of course be to remain in the present, however, if unresolved issues impact your present then you need to start at the root. We too often neglect our issues and trot forward as if they never occurred. Those of

21

us whose self identity is being held up by the thoughts and opinions of others could benefit from taking time to be by ourselves. It is in solitude where we are most uncomfortable most times, and this discomfort is a reaction to the world around us. So there is a lot of value in being uncomfortable. We wait too long to get to know the self and ask ourselves important questions so we can just *be*. We play the game created by the world around us and do it seriously. For once you don't place a burden on yourself and your expression, you will learn that everything is expression. And all you have to do is share with love.

Sometimes, the fear of being alone is caused by the lack of distractions present in solitude. Once someone finds comfort in who they are alone, anxiety caused by external interaction will tend to cease at least in proportion to the previous feeling. It is like losing a bond, and there is always value in a broken bond. It is when our props are removed that we actually become an individual. When people leave our life you see two things, your own value, or how much your value has been vested in the minds of others rather than your own. It is when we are vulnerable that we are able to see what we can be, not what we are told to be. All said should be done in moderation, I am in no way telling you to abandon all of those nearest you. Rather, ask yourself questions that lead you to finding yourself and examine the frame that contains you, to see the full picture.

Profound Pondering

"It's not solitude that we fear rather who we are in solitude that is feared"

FOUNDATIONS

The past

For one to make any stark reference to their present, they must first take time to explore their past. The events of the past when looked at from the present, have as much value as they have impact on us. If you were to not care for or invest value in a previous event, you'd have no reason to hold onto it. If we did not tie part of who we were to the ideas we were presented with in the past, then its impact would not be in question. However, many of the people who are aware that the past impacts the present understand that they don't know what has caused them undoing, until they look back. That is to say once we realize that we don't know what has caused us pain in the present we must look into the past. However, this is not to be mistaken with living in the past. This exploration is not something that we do to mitigate the past, it's to heal in the present. This search into the vast mind has no predetermined aggression towards the external world. Instead it is a deeply seeded curiosity to see the internal workings of all external expressions. The lack of ability to reference the past has made us at some points ungrateful for what we experience in the present. A man who was born with everything and retains it knows not the joy of acquiring what we never had. So in our everyday lives we must take moments to look back and realize the journey that has led us to this point. *It is one thing to realize everyone has their own complex life but it is entirely different to realize you have your own.*

Death

You only die once, yet you live every day. The fear of death is, at times, a mockery of the lives we live. To fear what is inevitable on a real scale, is to be negligent of the world around us and what is worth appreciating in our vicinity. To allow time to flow without us is impossible, we sadly just fail to take it into consideration that time is our perception of what is. It all means nothing, but its vacancy is what allows real meaning to exist. We don't have a lot of time to create an impact on the world before we depart, given the way we currently manage it.

The main point I'm trying to reach here is that death is what gives meaning to life. It is the realization that all will end that harmonizes madness, it's like a sick ruler that allows man to define what and where his meaning is stored in. The fact that every existence has no inherent meaning gives it meaning defined by each person who encounters it. I don't understand why, but absence breeds necessity; where there is a vacancy in the universe it begins to fill. However the way man works is different, the vacancy is caused by our own lack of perspective. What we do not see we forget and denote. We are selfish dictators to our own minds via our insistence that our way is the way. This idea permits only our own initial view to exist with certainty until we free ourselves from previous identification.

FOUNDATIONS

Our minds are our dictators. We in many ways have little to no control of our minds as we try to change our external more than our internal. We seek to change what we see instead of the person seeing it. This is not to say we have no chance, rather, we are the ones who have to provide it.

If it is to be

Traveling through life we are often presented with a plethora of options to channel our passion and energy into. To find a path is one thing, to stick to it is entirely different. In my experience with this philosophy even I have been lacking in expression or my pursuit in becoming what I wish to be. It's not as if I don't enjoy creation; rather, life gets ahead of us. work, Friends, and family all take up our time....Right? I think not, we often have a lot more time in our hands than we realize, we just fail to utilize it. Often, we are lazy or we push it off until later with the expectation our future self will be more willing. However, this is almost never the case, real change starts now and change is growth. Meaning that to grow we must start moving towards our growth now.

So why not? We have been programmed, I feel our value system is short lived. What has value gets validation in the world we see, and we think what we do and who we are has none when it receives no validation. Then, while being ourselves, tending towards our goals and aspirations seems like it's not worth it. Motivation is an essential part of achieving our goals. Something greater than ourselves brings forth the drive to achieve what at first seemed impossible. Motivation is great but unfortunately it does not last forever. What is left when our hard work bears no fruit? We stop or we regress to the state we were in before where nothing gets done. Or we choose to endure and prevail and the success we attain is thanks to what is known as discipline. The fuel that is left when the tank is empty. The realization that time must be sacrificed in order to gain what we never had. So the implication of any such thought is to press on seeking out our own goals and rid our minds of selfless narcissism where we sacrifice for all but ourselves. When you focus on what you genuinely and deeply desire, you create your own definition for life,

"If it is to be it's up to me" - Poppy (My Grandfather)

A SAFE HARBOR

In the pretext of natural life, we can seek comfort in what we already know. Instead of recognizing that there exist greater comforts within the unknown. From the moment we are born many statistics will plague us like mortality, disease, deformities, stress, anxiety, fear, etc. The meaning of our first life is to experience, and stagnation caused by comfort prohibits much of what each existence can offer. Comfort at times becomes a shackle to understanding, we trick ourselves into thinking that our current place in the world is the right one. It traps our identity in what we think we are rather than allowing us to transcend the labels of the past. One way I feel like comfort is built is in stereotypes and expectations. As a black man in my experience, I find that stereotypes are self-limiting. We are told we are less than, so once we are given a circumstance in which we are, we are okay with it. These engraved teachings are prohibitors of life, the more we think we know, the more we miss. I had first thought in school that I just wasn't one of the smart kids and for a time I was more than okay with this. However, there must come a day in this life when you demand better for yourself. A great quote from Jon Shedd states, "A ship in harbor is safe, but that's not why ships are built"[2]. That is to say safety and comfort are good things to possess, but the greatest comfort isn't where we are but who we are while there. Those who lead the path of discovery do not lie dormant and wait until

29

the harbor brings them treasure. They venture into both themselves and the world and see what exactly this world has to offer them. People will be themselves; find comfort in the change that benefits you wholly. Change is not to be feared for it is the one and only way to grow as people and become who you truly are.

Resilience

When living, the external world seems to constantly attempt to throw things in our path and set us astray from this unpredictable course. However, the defining characteristic of this undefinable course is that it cannot be defined. Each time we are forced to take a step in a direction we did not predict, we are learning to create the path that is us. Seeing problems in life is a part of being able to solve them. It's when our internal resilience is weak that external problems impact us most. To allow things to stab you from inside is confused servitude, for the perpetrator is always yourself. The bondage of self we face is only made possible and enforced through the mind's strength and our inability to see avenues to control it. It's only the mental image of the self that can be impacted, and it's tangible. Believing that you are the image is what makes you tangible. We are physically as we are, but the dysmorphia caused by negative thoughts is too much to remain in the mind as we are viewed in the world. We are subject to change, and this change, while at times external, is mainly a mental affair. We view our expressions as external, as do we with our resilience to the world.

We tend to keep our internal fluid and amiable via our lack of address of who we are, yet is this truly a negative thing? We should have parts of us open to the world's duality, but is this more harmful than good? Are we making ourselves victims yet again? or are we simply being human? Is it not within our nature to feel and experience? Is it not within our nature to be vulnerable? I think so, for we have what we are meant to have, whether that be in darkness or light. We are all that is under the sun. so the implication of which would push some to create a barrier for what you allow to change you. Instead, we should be likened to a filter for our expression and feelings as they pertain to the happenings of the external world. In other words, make a decision about who you are and how you will be expressed and stick to it. We must truly let the fire within burn brighter than all the flames around us; either way, we will be one. In this way, no barrier needs to be present in order to have stability within. We find that in our very efforts to defend ourselves from the world, we tend to attack ourselves.

THE LAW OF ATTRACTION

How much must we desire something before it falls into our possession? Is it the heavy desire that pushes it away? Do we attract what we obtain or are we just lucky to receive it? Is it like acting as if you have it to get it, or is it displaying your desire so greatly that it comes into being? At times I feel like I should have no worries and plunge myself into a reality where I act as if what has been sowed has already been reaped. Are we supposed to display gratitude for all that is? or simply treat ourselves as victims as we have before? If it has been done before, doing it again would be insane, so are we just expecting fruit before harvest? Should we wait and be patient as if we know the outcome or go and get this something? Are those the same? The law of attraction says that we must align our actions and feelings to attract what we desire. You must continue to plant seeds if you want to eat during the winter. How can one be sure that plants will bloom? Or is it the fact that we've seen it happen that we are not skeptics? So, should we trust in ourselves? Why? What has been shown in truth that would allow such an instantiation to be grounded in soundness? *Is soundness even attainable if it's us who contain the uncertainty?* I am in search of the answer, so we must know we don't know all. Which means there must be things that we have faith in. We all experience things we don't know the explanation for. Life is fragile and tangible, do we make the choice to move forward or is there something that is driving our action? To attract anything, we must begin to treat ourselves with the validity and value of already having that something. When we approach the world from a mentality of lack, lack is what we tend to see and experience. We see in the world what we carry in our hearts, and if we never carry that which we want at least in feeling, we won't attract it into our lives. Action is a great catalyst to attraction, as at times we must begin to show ourselves what we wish for the world to show us.

WHAT SHOULD I BE DOING?

With the modern work and dream aspiring culture, many fail to cultivate their own desires. Better yet, do we fail to cultivate our own dreams? Is it given or learned? Do we drop everything for it or are dreams too intangible for us to trust fully? What should I be doing is a question that many of us ask daily. In a place like college, I've been able to notice a lot of what I lack, knowing that, how are we supposed to just...Improve? How does the knowledge of a vacancy help it become filled? Are we fueled by what we lack or what we desire? In life, we all have many experiences that shape who we are and how we approach the unknown. So, if a desire is created out of absence, how genuine are the actions of man? We are but victims to our environment, or is it something greater? And something that gets me is the distance between our mind's desire and our physical reality, how patient is too patient? And what comes from thoughts of impatience? Is it like the law of attraction that the distance perceived in our minds causes things to take more time to be attained or are things outside of the domain of vibration? Are we preordained to do something or does the concept of fate rid man of free will or expression? Can we do anything? How large is the setback needed to give up on ambition? Peace is allowing the mind to come into play when needed, not when provoked. In this way we can learn to create exactly what we desire both in feeling and in action. In a current address of what should I be doing? I would say that awareness is the answer, vacancy can only be filled through a conscious action. And our desires can only be worked towards if we give ourselves the ground we stand on. As you become present enough to know how you feel and what you want. What am I doing can be answered as soon as you look in front of you

<u>What place do I have in this world</u>

If the question takes away the answer

The our curiosity is misplaced

For if I am not here

Who will stand in my space

We understand the world

But we don't the self

And if we are part of what we inhabit

Then we lose more than our health

The light of self knowing

Akin to the sun

We ask

What place do I have in this world?,

This one

YOU CAN'T HEAL FROM WHAT YOU DON'T ACKNOWLEDGE

To tend to any wound, we must first accept that a wound is present. Too often in life I feel we get caught up in maintaining an image of our strength. So much so that we forget to take care of what causes us pain. Real strength is not never being injured, but rather constantly healing from whatever life has to throw in your direction. And many times, we are the very ones who throw these things in our direction, as our life is our own. Concerning ourselves, our wounds are very much the same. A great deal of our mental ambiguity is caused by our inability to accept who we are, as well as give ourselves the necessary validation to heal from the lack we receive from the world. If we spend all of our time focused on what takes place around us, we lose all that is within us. That is to say that we cannot always live our lives in reference to that which is not us. We as people often create fictitious images of ourselves in our heads. These images create an unrealistic ideal for the world around us. It is the way that we separate ourselves in our minds from ourselves in reality that creates anxiety of self. We spend so much time wondering who we are that we forget we are here. *It's almost as if the very question of ourselves creates a lack of answer*. What are my current actions tending to? Who can I define myself as at this moment? We must open our eyes and see that we exist right here, and the answers to our questions are here as well. You can't understand who you are, without experiencing who you are. You can't experience who you are if you fail to be present enough to see it. *You don't become someone, you are someone, you just become more aware.*

If we are the root of our suffering, then we must also be the root of all that is good to us. We just have to be mindful enough to nurture that which is going to benefit us wholly and morally. Just as an ignored wound is likely to become infected, an unacknowledged self is likely to become corrupted. Love for anything and especially the self should be without condition, so why make yourself jump over hurdles before you learn to appreciate what you are. I assure you, what you are is enough and it always has been. If you always live in reference to an ideal self or something that isn't you, how can you ever be the subject of your own life. If you're always looking back how can you ever take steps forward, especially if you can't acknowledge where you are?

LOVE YOUR EMBODIMENT, NOT JUST THE EXPRESSION

We as people contain many sides to our character and many things that comprise what we know to be the self. One of the most prominent of which is the Ego, a necessary something we need in order to express who we are. The Ego is connoted as something we must rid ourselves of, and something that is inherently negative. However, I think that there are just negative expressions of ego created by lack of awareness of who we are internally. *Who we are is not the expression of who we are, but the thing that is expressing it.* We spend so much of our lives playing out a character until we realize that it's something that we are *playing.* That's not to say who we are is fake, rather, how we are expressed is up to our perspective of the world around us and more so our relationship to said perspective. If you cannot love the embodiment, any expression will be void of love. If you cannot love who you are behind your expression then no matter how you express yourself, part of you will find discomfort. We need to learn how to love our foundation so whatever we build upon is filled with us and not just our ideas. The Ego, at times, is the personification of the mind and not truth, it's how we are able to attach ourselves to that which is not us. The Ego can connect us to many things in the world. However, it often is the cause of our separation. It is because we feel so individual that we act as such, but it's not about feeling like an individual, it's about

39

acting like one. To have love for yourself is in many ways to have love for the world because we are not separate. The same goes for others, not to say be solely selfless to other people's complexities rather, be mindful of your own enough to recognize theirs.

While realizing we have our own complex life we must also accept that other people have their own. Not to say be narcissistic or selfish to others but have some selflessness for yourself and your understanding. Allowing yourself to be is about reaching beyond how you interact with the world and focusing on how you interact with yourself. Have love for what you do and how you express yourself, but more importantly have love for who is expressing it.

Blade of Grass

If you could point above you'd see worry

If you could point behind you'd see nothing new

To point below is to think its dead

And to point ahead is to live what's said

The blade of grass

Only cuts the space in our mind

For if it's not occupied by us

Then it's occupied by time

HOW TO GROW

Is there a guaranteed way to grow? How can we be sure that what we are doing for our growth is effective? Once we decide to start working on the self, we become shrouded by the many realizations that surround our idea. These ideas at times can cause a person to feel as if they are growing inversely. It's almost as if by committing ourselves to our improvement, we see the many things we can improve. What we alter however, is growth, and this presents the question: is all change growth? I believe so, growth does not always have to be, nor is it at all times, a positive thing. We are akin to plants; however, we place ourselves at times not in bad soil, but in negative ideas. Especially within the idea that all of our issues must be solved in order for us to see our growth. For growth is not a matter of potential, but present realization.

The only way to continue to see growth is to continue to encounter parts of ourselves that seek out change. Not to say change in reference to the world around you, but most definitely to change in proportion to the self. Not limiting our growth and change to external factors, rather allowing yourself to be a factor in how you wish to change. Many of the problems in our minds are confined within it. That is to say, we often suffer more than necessary by suffering in our mind prior to real events in the world. We are stuck in an interesting inbetween which consists of being both the viewer, and thing being viewed. When we don't acknowledge this position, we neglect the ways at which our perspective of who we are, is the most limiting factor in our growth. There are many objectives that a person may seek, however the most vital ones are not of the external world, but the person within it. Most of all growth is found in accepting your own role as someone responsible for yourself and all you bring. Growth is constant. We as people must make the active choice to get better, especially if we want our betterment to unfold as we wish.

Growth isn't about the nature of the world and its reaction to us, it's about the nature of the self and our reaction to the world. Many times, our growth is characterized by our ability to create reference within the self. This means we create reference points to previous memories of who we were, being able to set a steady foundation in the self in the present for it to flourish. If we can accept that positivity and negativity both exist, then we must take responsibility for what we wish to bring in and pour out of ourselves. *The world is only as it is, and our perception of it is only as we allow it to be.* Your growth is always a matter of you and you, and once you realize that, all you have to do to grow is continue to be you wholly.

LETTING GO IS WHAT MAKES IT STAY

Why do we treat our negativity as something we must escape from, and our positivity like something we must hold onto? The very principles which we address ourselves with work against us. When referencing our negative aspects, it is as if we try to run from the parts of ourselves that are seeking out change. The notion of having to run from negativity implies that if we were to sit still, it would catch us. As if our negativity is inherent to our character so much so, that we must constantly combat it. Positivity on the other hand, and our good aspects at times seem fleeting enough for us to think they need to be held onto. As if letting ourselves go would rid our nature of its positivity. The problem here isn't that we have positive and negative, rather, that we think our good is not part of us, and that our negativity is. Letting go is what makes it stay is to say that when we do find those things we like about ourselves, *allow* them to be part of you. The easiest acknowledgement of this would be to let it go. Letting go because, if those characteristics are really part of you, then they wouldn't leave, even when you let go. Our power as people has never in my opinion been in what we hold, but in what we have. It's about what comes with you, not what you attempt to bring. which is not to say you can't add more to yourself and broaden your idea. It's to say that you don't need to hold on tightly to yourself because you will always be there.

When practicing anything developmental, the stress should not be within constantly thinking about its implementation, but to be present enough to have the choice. If I want to be more patient, I don't constantly stress myself with the idea of my patience. I choose to be present enough to embody that which I want to be a part of myself. When talking about running from our negativity, the inverse should be applied. Letting it go as if it's not something that can ever catch us, because what it is, is not us, so long as we are present enough to make the choice. What we accept as a part of us, becomes a part of us.

COMPARISON

If we allow ourselves to live in reference to everything around us, we will never be free of our own expectations. The main issue that we face within the world is our pursuit of self, or lack thereof. Life is a search for worth and learning to find it inside yourself, instead of the world around you. The difficulty with finding internal value is waiting on something other than yourself to place that value. Spending so much of our time living in the mind. we too become subject to its bias. Within this world of the mind, we fail to permit ourselves an audience enough to actually be within the world. This is because we are stuck performing. Sometimes the act of shifting your intention to yourself, and doing things for yourself, allows you to live. Comparison being the thief of joy is a saying which contains much truth, Joy can only be experienced by you. If what you are is only found in your comparisons to others, then your joy will always be outside of you. Of course, certain things are strengthened by contrast, however in that same way, we don't judge yellow for not being blue, We shouldn't judge ourselves for not being others. In being an active participant, we give ourselves the greatest gift that can be given, opportunity. The more present we allow ourselves to be, the more we will be able to see what we can benefit from in just being ourselves. Not to say work does not need to be done to gain, but to say *discipline is self-love*. It's a subtle realization that if we are to do anything to gain, we must be the ones to do it. And if what we are doing is in a way for us, then what we are is beyond comparison.

BEGIN AT ONCE

If we can relax our minds enough to melt into the moment, we will be at peace with all that we are. Our endeavor is only as great as we are weak, and we are typically only weak in thought. Our strength as people is not derived from how impervious we are to life's tribulations. Rather, how much we are able to heal from the wounds that life inflicts upon us. The beauty of this experience is not in our effort, rather in our acceptance, as to live is to embrace possibility. Giving yourself a chance at a chance or allowing yourself to pursue that which seems to be beyond you. All that we do tends towards us, our ideas, our identity, and most of all, our wholeness. *He who thinks the journey is over is truly lost in this way*. The pursuit of self is something that acts at times as an undercurrent in our actions. This is because who we are is very much vested in what we value outside of who we are. In saying that our endeavor is only as strong as we are weak, our strength is what allows things to be overcome. For if we were strong, any obstacle would cease to be an obstacle and become yet another step towards more strength. *The greatest challenge isn't what we encounter, but how we encounter ourselves through it*. Moving forward takes you, leaving yourself behind at times. Not in a sense of leaving behind who you are, rather realizing that there's much more to discover. Who you are is meant to be renewed and grown into something ever more beautiful. A way of being which contains all that is old yet makes it new once again. Everything is new, and today always marks the start of the future.

So, to begin at once is to embrace the possibility of possibility, for we lose nothing in trying yet gain everything in success. The point isn't to live in the possibility of defeat or failure, for we can always lose. If success is a mentality, then the successful are those who place themselves beyond the possibility of defeat. *There is no room for doubt when we are attempting to do that which has yet to be done. For if it has, you already know of its possibility.*

FOUNDATIONS

THE PAST HAS PASSED

The saying, *let yesterday be yesterday,* is not to neglect what was, rather, *embrace what is.* Once we allow our viewpoint to come from where we are, we are more apt to see where we want to go. In the present moment we find both our goals, and the person who is going to carry them. This is to say that it is important to vest your value where you are, not where you have been previously. Circumstances naturally impact our world view; however this does not mean we have no impact on ourselves. Once you award yourself with a certain degree of awareness, you allow change to truly occur for your benefit. For it is not just intention that places things in the world for us, but action. To act in a real sense, is to be present enough with your desires to actually act upon them. When we get into periods of improvement, many of us fail to make lasting change. We spend some time changing or at least feeling as if we are, until we realize we are back to who we used to be. This is not a terrible thing, however, to make lasting change we have to learn to not only change our perspective on the world and the past, *but on the present and ourselves.* How you view yourself is how you view the world. If we do not take the proper time to accept who we were in the past, and who we are now, then we will never be able to accept the world around us. Our comfort is in a way dependent on our ability to be comfortable with our internal present. For when we are uncomfortable, we don't experience much more than our own feelings and thoughts about what might be.

    This is not to say be neglectful of potential dangers or force yourself into uncomfortable situations. This is to say figure out ways you make yourself uncomfortable, by not granting yourself release from the past. If we want to move forward, we must leave certain things behind. Not ridding them of value, rather realizing that we don't have to value ourselves based on who we were in the past. We can begin at once to reestablish and start over in our journey of self and figuring out who we are. A lot of people might like the idea of a new year. However, each day is an opportunity for renewal, the past has passed, and we need to let it do so.

FOUNDATIONS

<u>Seeing past yourself</u>

I'm Tired

Tired of the way all around me is me

Not to say that I am everything

But I allow everything to be me

Projection of my blundering

And my negativity come to light

Lost in a battle with self

There is no option other than fight

the self isn't something we leave

For what we run from has already caught us

And if we run from what we seek

Then how can we ever be found

So we cower into the mind, in the world

Worried about all that keeps our mind in itself whirl

Not realizing the world is pure as a pearl

Only if we allow it to be outside of the swirl

Profound Pondering

The spins of the mind do so with ease

Because it's our focus on leaves

That makes us forget the trees

That make us forget the forest in bloom

So of course we aren't free

We haven't even left our rooms

Not every closed door is locked

We all at times must push

But escape from the mind doesn't need effort

It is a gentle bush

And if we tend to it properly, we will never be shushed

Silenced by that we wish to silence

We must allow to allow

And allow to see

For everything around is only it

And I am only me

Section Two:

Fluidity

Is there any one set way a person should be?

There are often many beliefs which serve to limit who we are and how we can be. In our address of self, we must give ourselves real room to be free and be as we are. It's not what contains us, but what we contain within ourselves that truly binds us.

Profound Pondering

IF WE WERE TO JUST TRY

If we were to try, we would see that what we are isn't defined by failure or success. It's defined by the way we attempt to obtain that which has yet to come into our possession. We are what we put into life, as life is not what you see, life what you are. Our effort towards the lives we live, if done properly, is not effort at all. Instead, a proclamation of the love you have for yourself. We all contain dualities within, but no separation is reason enough to detach love from yourself. Everyone can fail, just as we all can succeed, and *to know it's humanly* possible *means you too can do it*[13]. You can do anything you desire; however, this takes you actually taking part in the doing. *Why keep your dreams in your head if you want them in reality.* Our dreams will remain in your head until we put them into reality. Failure to fail is not success, for if you never try you've already failed at giving yourself a chance at success. It is sometimes an act of love to fail; it's to give yourself new glasses which allow you to see yourself for what you have, rather than what you lack. Who we are is both the experience and the unknown, mixed into an orientation you refer to as yourself. To accept the possibility of not knowing is to open yourself to the lesson present. When we allow ourselves to live in the unknown, we begin to know more. This is to say that when you open your perspective enough to see the world, instead of only seeing yourself, you will learn about both. Sometimes when

55

we are present, we are awarded a perspective that sees life for what it is, rather than what we are. This can be either good or bad, but *if you don't open yourself to what is, it'll never be what you want it to be.*

To say you can't heal what you don't acknowledge is to say that if we fear our negativity, we will never be able to gain what is positive. If we run from what is seeking out change, we will always be caught by what we wish to escape from, ourselves. This is why I think the importance here would be to try. To give yourself enough to exist in the world around you and allow it to be the world around you. When we derive our sense of value from what we possess; we lose all we can gain from being ourselves. No one thing is forever, especially if you are based on something that is fleeting. If we are able to see ourselves as the foundation to our value, then our value will only be as scarce as we aren't present.

Peace

    Happiness is not pleasure, it's *peace*. Too often we mistake boredom or lack of stimulation as a problem. Causing our minds to attach to the many abstractions that exist within it, placing our attention anywhere but the present moment. The thing that takes away our natural flow of creativity is our lack of appreciation for peace. We become clouded by our desire for stimulation, by our inability to regard *silence* as a comfortable sound. Which causes our free time to be used to escape from ourselves, rather than meeting ourselves. In doing this, we diminish our capacity for directed attention and controlled action, primarily towards that which we genuinely desire.

    With shorter attention spans our interactions with the real world suffer in silence. Conversations where you could talk for hours about your innermost desires, viewpoints, and feelings seem pointless. We have a strange fast track system of value, where we always believe that something must be gained in order to have value. We have been taught that in our relationships we must always be receiving something, in order for it to be sustained. It is this notion that something must be gained, that is actually stripping away the happiness of life. This peace that is spoken of is the absence of worrying about the world, through the self. In our repetitive address of the world's negativity, we make no real contrast great enough to breed happiness. As joy is not living without pain but realizing that pain was never supposed to stop our joy. If happiness is to be based on pleasure, we would also have to undergo things that make us unhappy for it to be sustained. For pleasure and pain are two sides of the same coin. And the middle path, which is peace, is peace from the beginning to end of its scale.

When our peace goes unacknowledged, the boredom created by a lack of problems will inevitably be too much. Many will once again plunge into our issues, by allowing them to be inconsistent with our peace. We at times seek out problems in a way to take a certain amount of attention away from the self. Some of us can see the value contained within peace, and we must pressure ourselves to see it within. Some kind of pressure must be added in order to create an identity that is ready to handle the world around us. Some people identify so much with these issues that they don't know what they would be without them. We make the mistake of saying that we crave peace while walking into an area of war. We ourselves, drink the poison we are trying to find the antidote for.

Pain

When referencing the hardships of life, we must first define what a hardship is. Is a hardship just when things do not go our way? Or is it something much deeper? A while ago when talking about how we define identity, I said that all we are is the reaction to our environment. I still believe this to be mostly true, to live is to interact, and to interact is to react. To change as people, we often don't change anything but our reactions, which allow our actions to follow. With that mindset you could theoretically change who you are externally in a matter of seconds.

So why don't we?

In a podcast with some friends we argued about this topic, about whether or not a person could change who they were in a short amount of time. The consensus was that you could not immediately change. Society and all the life leading up to your *now* won't allow you to abandon yourself. In other words, our conformance with our ego has halted any speedy progress, without its direct acknowledgement. Which is why I believe mental illness is so prevalent amongst us. We play our roles until we realize we are playing them, then the realization that we are stuck as this person breeds depression. The feeling that we no longer want to be ourselves or to no longer exist. When referencing emotions, I can be noted saying that we should not suppress them, or that letting go will take away their

59

control over you. To some extent this information is true, however I never really thought about how valuable emotions are to the creation of an identity.

Even when we are describing others, we attach a general mood or emotion to them so as to better define their character. With reference to pain, many of us identify with our trauma. Kahlil Gibran once said," Your pain is the breaking of the shell that encloses your understanding, even as the stone of the fruit must break, that is heart may stand in the sun, so you must know pain"[3]. That is to say if we conform to our pain then once something tells us otherwise then we tend to feel it. He is also saying that this sort of pain is characteristic of the human experience, seeing as pain is only the reaction to the absence of freedom within identity. To know joy, you must at first know pain, to be free you must know what it is to be stuck.

So why do we speak of pain as if we want it gone, yet hold onto it like it defines us. It's almost as if we are asking others for help, for a problem that we always run back to. We are in some ways the physician and the patient all at once. You as you are, being both the solution and the cause of our own undoing. "Before you heal someone, ask him if he's willing to give up the things that make him sick" - Hippocrates. The problem here is we don't confront our issue, *we run from it with the expectation that we'll outrun it, but we are just running from ourselves.*

Reducing ones stress

As we play out these roles, we must at times see how stressful the world can be if we only look from a glance. In a matter of seconds, our minds and perspectives can shift into the negative aspects of life. The inquiry present is, what is the plausible justification to stress ourselves over that which is outside of our control? The main person we should watch over is ourselves. For "Under peaceful conditions the warlike man will attack himself"[4]- Friedrich Nietzsche. Even when we exist in "comfort" our minds are inclined to find discomfort in the world around us. We are known to hold grudges and allow others to control our emotions. However, people are just people, and it's the connotation of our own mind that allows or permits others entry. We have no enemies, only ideas, the man who hates gains that capacity from his own understanding and relation to himself. The more deeply we know ourselves, the more deeply we can connect with others. Expression should not be a forced thing; it should be an allowed thing. To eliminate the corruption of the mind, we must start by living in the moment and in our bodies. What I mean by this is to listen to yourself, fact check your mind. That's how you free yourself from some of the stress the world has to offer. It's also the association with the ego that causes stress, we try to maintain an image, instead of recognizing that there is no image to be maintained, but a person to be.

Fluidity

To protect yourself from such suffering, focus on the present moment. However, *do not add to it* just see, listen, just be here, wholly, rather than in the mind. For the mind is not external, rather a projection of our internal world onto our reality. For how we feel in an internal sense will always be found within our external perspective. Control your own focus to focus, do not reject the mind itself, use it as a tool. Intelligence in some ways is not all mental.

Profound Pondering

THE CHANGE OF THE SEASONS

In times past, the tide of the seasons has caused many of us pain, as change in our environment stimulates change in the mind. Especially when part of our security is based on the world we see. We get comfortable in certain circumstances and feel like it's ripped from under our feet. The true seasons we as people often experience, however, are not external. We can see within ourselves changes of mood and even the mindsets that lead us toward changing our circumstances. However, at times we find ourselves stuck on a certain aspect of the season past and attempt to stay stagnant with it. There exist certain occurrences that have you puzzled for days or, have you stuck in hypothetical thought which prohibit the mind from being used to our own advantage. The lives we live should be for our own benefit, not to always appease those around us, rather to appease them by being who we are fully. The creation of one's own season is brought forth through personal development. We hardly ever take ourselves into account and ask ourselves how we truly feel. Instead, we convince ourselves we feel a certain way. Allowing the logic of false analysis of our own psychology, to limit how and what we feel. And while we are impacted by our thoughts, we are not the thought of ourselves, we are ourselves. Be careful what image you carry, the more you stress and hold onto it, the greater it will change your current perception of life. To not allow the external to

63

impact you is quite difficult in my experience. At some points, I must reject some of my mind's own influence. Seeing the causes of your suffering is only part of the puzzle we call life. It's understanding why it caused you suffering that has a greater meaning. Understanding what causes you pain is one of the only ways to see how to create joy in your own life.

DERIVING SELF WORTH

How do we self-worth? What is the worth of self? Moreso, does that sort of thing exist past what we know as ego? Are we attached to this image because we like it? Or do we like it because we find ourselves being attached to it? I think ideas of self-worth start when we are young, and depending on our circumstances/environment, we can expose ourselves to certain energies that influence how we develop as people. However, once the self becomes conscious, it's a little more of a detriment. It can seem as if you've wanted attention your whole life, only to realize that you needed to give some to yourself the whole time. If things like this are hard to articulate and ask for, how can we expect that out of ourselves, the stress of worth is unrealistic. "How can I, a man of young age, truly derive worth from my existence? I have yet to do much, and I am not crazily ahead of those around me". This is the point exactly, *the way we wish is too much based on application instead of being.* Things should and do have value just by being there. We need to understand and gather who we are to get that kind of worth. I feel like some of the pains of existence fool the mind, we are beautiful regardless of what society states. Self-worth should not be based on status, rather strength and goodness of character. So, value the self without reference. value the self because it is possible.

RELAXATION

Do we ever appreciate the effort it takes to be ourselves? Do we take for granted the life we've been given by not living it? Many people die before they allow themselves to live. The life we live is filled with ambiguity, which is a great opportunity to exert your own influence upon yourself. Many find that since life has no inherent meaning, we are permitted with an opportunity to ascribe our own. Life is uncertain at all points, so why not use the space we occupy to do as much as we can? The flow of life isn't about not doing anything, but using conscious effort to do what you desire, and not allowing your mind to get in your way. It's about building the proper structure, so eventually it takes no conscious effort to be the best version of yourself. Many of our thoughts are never able to leave the mind's restrictions. *We are caged by the very thing that makes us feel most free.* The way at which we attain meaning is not through introspection, rather, perception. Is this negative? The life we are given is founded on some external interaction, so to react internally some external stimulus is needed. So, we must take action. We too often try to relax without taking the time to truly do so. *When you genuinely do the work, and put yourself into your actions, then you are able to put yourself into your relaxations.* Time is something infinite yet limited for the life we share. It's so abundant and yet we find ourselves not having enough of it to satisfy our desires.

Profound Pondering

Work at times only feels like work due to the system we set up into our own minds. We have a certain expectation that contradicts our desires, creating a space where we cannot work without the fruits of our labor being present. Relaxation isn't an action, it's a reward for putting effort into your development, whether it be physical or mental. Life is meant to be lived, not looked for.

COMPARISONs

Life is meant to be lived, not looked for. Taking all external circumstances into your internal self is making you a victim to yourself. We are supposed to take in and give more than we analyze. The more time we spend focusing on things that are not us, the more of the self we lose. We need to take the time to realize how much we can contribute to who we are. It is not because we are individuals that we are special, but because we are special that we are individuals. Part of life is realizing that everyone has their own complex life. This being said, I think it's also extremely important to realize you have your own. "Comparison is the thief of joy", to base oneself off of what we lack is worthless, *we will always lack as long as we have more to gain.* That is to say that it is not about acknowledging what you do not have, rather making sure you show appreciation for what you do have. The thing that we should have in our possession most of all, is ourselves. The world contains too much for it to be a battle versus yourself. It was never supposed to be you vs. you, *instead it should be you and you.* Treating yourself like you would a friend, and holding yourself accountable, are some of the only ways to have yourself in full. No one person can take up the space that you do or see the world from your perspective. Which is not to say disregard the thoughts of others, but to regard the thoughts that you have. There is no person who is you other than you, there are no grounds for comparison.

Fluidity

You don't need to Hold on

We hold on to a plethora of things that have no way to serve who we are. There are many issues and endeavors we allow to linger in our minds, without real reference to how things truly are. The way I see it we drink the very poison that makes us sick, in the hope that one day it will be the antidote. At times we indulge in thoughts and actions that are the cause of the same pain we wish to be free from. A large amount of issues cannot be simply over thought through. Overthought places sometimes false meaning in events that often do not require any speculation. The things we choose to dwell on, at times, do nothing but take up space in our hearts and minds. In some ways, we allow our feelings to convince us to make personal, what is not inherent to our character in the slightest. Not to say that emotions are negative at all, rather how we feel governs, in some ways, how we see the world and vice versa. The sooner we come to this realization, the sooner we can truly heal. Part of letting go is accepting what is, and still appreciating what is left for you to experience. Otherwise, you live in a world void of yourself, *if you're always living in reference how can you be the subject of your own life?* We hold onto the things that cause us pain, often in expectation that something will magically change its nature because we think it should. If all we can do in a situation is think about it, then thinking of something else may be to our benefit. The tool that is the mind solves most issues.

Profound Pondering

When you give it something that is only grounded in your mind's bias and your lack of self-validation, you start looking for yourself in things that aren't you.

Peace is one of the best things for us—not peace as in happiness, rather tranquility of self. We lose a lot of who we are, in our obsession about things that we are not. If we only look at what is outside, we will fail to process all that we have within. What is within is what we allow our minds to be stuck with, our reality in many ways is governed by how we view the world, and more importantly, how we view ourselves.

Fluidity

<u>Being</u>

If we only think

Then our dreams are more mind

Then water is drink

Some may be mean and some kind

For duality exists in the mind

To be in your dream

Is to be in the world

To be in the world

Is not how it seems

For there is no world without dreams

Lost in thought

 a cage of freedom

When you don't like yourself

So, you want to be them

You say you aren't sufficient

Well, that's fine

For your value only exists

In the mind

THE MOST ADJACENT STEP

The troubles of life are often caused by our inability to confront our relationship to our issues. We often attribute to self, that which is outside of us in an attempt to validate our own perspective of the world. What I think we fail to realize, is that our perspective of the world is a reflection of how we view ourselves. I say this not to say that "there's no bad in the world, just ourselves" or something like that. We often contribute to our own negativity a lot more than we realize. If we fail to see things for what they are, they become what we are, and often that is unacknowledged. The more we fail to see ourselves, the more we fail to see what is right in front of us, and vice versa. Ultimately, we cannot heal what we do not acknowledge. Therefore, if we ourselves are not seen, then we'll never be healed. Our presence and audience with the self is vital to our progression as people. The progression of self is not characterized by our ability to see how we relate to the world, rather, how we relate to ourselves. This isn't done all in a day or some short amount of time, rather done at each step of the path. When it comes to our goals and growth it's important to walk the path, instead of chasing the outcome. If what we are looking for is ourselves, then we will always be lost. The only place we find ourselves is where we are. The first step always reveals the second, and if we take the time to step into ourselves, then there's no limit to who we can become.

NOTHING OUTSIDE OF YOU DETERMINES YOUR VALUE

We spend so much time attempting to gain possessions to show us that we are valuable. Without realizing, we are the ones who give value to that which makes us "valuable". That is to say, we invest so much of who we are in things that we are not. We do this in expectation that these things will show us more of what we are, when they only can show more of what they are. Our view of ourselves is represented in our view of the world, or more so, our entire experience. When we tend our minds to the moment, and embrace some sort of affirmation of the self, we find that the moment is always filled with what we give to ourselves. We spend so much time trying to see the life around us that we forget we are the life we experience. If we are unable to give ourselves fully to the moment, then there is no moment to experience in the first place. If we wait for the world to tell us we are valuable after it experiences us; then who we are is more focused on being experienced than actually experiencing. To say that nothing outside of you determines your value, is really to say that you are your value. The only place that you can find yourself is where you are. Therefore, your value is always with you. Some often remark that the world is bleak or empty, *without knowing they must fill it with themselves.*

Profound Pondering

If we can accept ourselves, we can accept the world. Which is not to say you'll agree with everything; Rather, to say that you won't be moved by your own disagreement. What is outside will be more of itself because you will be more of yourself. If we don't see things for what they are, we will see them for what we are. If what we are is not filled with value, positivity, and whatever love we have for ourselves, then it will not be in the world we experience. So, in a way, to see any value in the world is to in part see it in yourself. If you see anything beautiful in the world around you, *you too must contain that beauty.*

YOUR PERSONAL WORLD

If you could have it your way, I doubt you'd let yourself live in the world of your own negativity. Once we truly see ourselves, we can truly seek what we desire. If we are unable to grant ourselves an audience, then we will be too stuck in our performance, to actually explore our character. *I think the real importance of our life is to better understand how to interact with the self, not with the world.* At times we will come to a realization that we are undoing ourselves in our effort to be who we are not. When we allow ourselves to be prominent within our own viewpoint, seeing is no longer about what you are viewing, rather the way you view it. We need to better understand that not all thoughts contribute to who we are, and not all perspectives accommodate us as well as our own. This is not to say embrace and care only for yourself and your viewpoint, but to say grant yourself space to truly grow. The people we are, tend to be irreplaceable to the extent that we are beyond comparison. No one can compete where they do not compare, and we tend to compare everything to ourselves. In this way, instead of being ourselves we become everything around us.

Our doubt, however, always keeps us in a state of displacement. The more we doubt ourselves, the more we question who we are, and the more we question, *the less available the answer is.* We have to understand that how we see ourselves, in a way, is how we view the world. So, if we desire to live in a world that accommodates us, we must first take the time to accommodate ourselves. Your personal world is one where you don't have to try to be yourself or try to understand who you are. Instead, you allow, for _we don't learn in effort but in willingness to listen._

IF YOU DON'T WANT TO REPEAT THE PAST, BE PRESENT

The only place where you can begin to change who you are is where you are. This is to say that our overzealous effort to escape the past is at times unwarranted. We focus too much on what has occurred while trying to create something that we call "new". In this way, we lose our very ability to truly create, *if we only reference the past when building the future, all we will do is recreate it*. Who we were and the moments we often reference no longer exist, the only thing that we are, is right now. This is not to say that if you've done something in the past it did not happen. Rather, when we want to overcome past parts of ourselves, the importance is acknowledgement, not repetition. When we live in our previous feelings about ourselves, we perpetuate them. We in this way are bringing them into the present moment and once again, making the past present. I think that the importance is to let yesterday be yesterday and let today be filled with whatever you choose. To say if you don't want to repeat the past, be present, is in reference to this idea. When we keep our mind centered around the past, then our current self will have no choice to exemplify the exact feeling we are trying to escape from. What we run from has already caught us in this way, and we cannot keep running from the things we wish to overcome. If one wishes to move past anything, it first takes them actually facing that which they wish to overcome. I find that when

78

we run from these issues or these parts, we aren't running from anything but ourselves. For you are the only thing that you can never escape. I mean this not to be pessimistic, rather, hopeful.

If we can recognize that the self will always be there, then the importance isn't to get rid of anything. Instead, turn it into something you are comfortable having around, *as long as you have yourself you have someone*. The positivity and the love we share for ourselves in the present moment is what creates a future filled with it. What we give to ourselves in this way, is what we experience. So, if we want to live in a world that is better than the past, the importance isn't in just seeing the good around you. The good is in seeing the current and potential good within yourself.

RETURN TO SELF

When our goal is to be who we are, constant reference to the past is often used. In the same way when we are attempting to become new and improve upon what is, we use this past as some sort of point of reference. In placing who we are in reference, I feel we unknowingly limit our ability to actually grow into who we wish to become. Not because the past is not worth looking at, rather realizing that who you are is already where you are. The best way to change your current self is to be able to see who you currently are, in both thought and in action. The focus on the past is likely to cause repetition, as we become accustomed to the feelings and thoughts that were shared by the previous versions of who we are. A return to yourself isn't about going back to who we were in the past, rather coming back into the moment, to see who you are now and what you wish to be. *The most paradoxical thing about change is you can only truly do it once you accept yourself as you are.* When we don't return to the present moment, in regard to our change, then we tend to be victims of previous circumstances. *Trying to apply change to what was, rather than what is.* This is not to say that the past has no impact on who you are currently, however our efforts need to be directed into the now. In terms of healing, we must acknowledge that which we wish to heal. In acknowledging the past, we open the door to healing, but when we live in the past, that change becomes stagnation.

Profound Pondering

Our inability to be present with our ailments makes them in a way chronic. If we don't take the time to sit still with the motion inside us, then the cycle will be as repetitive as we are human.

The cycles in life I find are only as cyclic as we allow them to be. We keep making the same choices mentally, physically, and spiritually, that keep us in the same identity that we wish to grow from. Our growth in this way is only as grand as we are open to change in our perspective. If we can give ourselves enough space, then we will be able to grow. When we keep the *same mentality about ourselves, we keep the same reality.*

AVOIDANCE IS MORE HARMFUL THAN THE PROBLEM ITSELF

Our own hysteria surrounding our problems is often more negatively experienced than the problem itself. The more we embellish ourselves in thoughts which do not contribute to the lives we live, the more we cease to live a life we desire. Not to say life becomes without value or meaning, rather, instead of being within our own definition, our value is defined by the world around us. The role of avoidance in our lives is a subtle undercurrent which does nothing but shelter us from ourselves. Many times, the problems we face are our own internal issues, rather than real external problems. It is always about the relationship that our identity has to any given circumstance, which defines how we tend to experience it. This is to say that when we take a step forward from our own identification with our problems, they cease to be problems. It truly is about accepting things as they are, so you can in a real way, be as you are. When we allow ourselves to only live in reference, then we cannot act out of accordance with the role we force ourselves to play. If we don't give ourselves any audience, then we will perform until we get accolades from those who watch us, rather than ourselves. To say avoidance is more harmful than the problem, is to extend a hand to yourself to overcome what is in front of you. The more we try to hide from what we face, the more it tends to seek us out in the perspective we take on the world around us. Even if we are able to push something away from the forefront of our mind. *What we run from has already caught us.*

I find that once we let our guard down against what is, we begin to attack what was. Your best bet or opportunity in overcoming what has happened in the past, is by being in the now. To be present in this way, is to prove to yourself that your peace is not determined by anything but you. Letting go of our necessity for events to go in our favor or for the world to be a certain way, allows you to fulfill your own requirements. *What the world doesn't give to you, you must learn to give to yourself.* How can you overcome an obstacle you never interact with? How can you ever change the way you desire, if you never look at the thing you are trying to change?

Fluidity

Hello from now

How can one be lost on a search for self

It's as if he know he's the cure, yet still questions his health

If he were to let go of that which makes him sick

Then he would be as healed as he is

For he was never sick, "I" was

And until we understand

I will already be, lost in an effort to find

The human condition

If only we find what we look for

We'd stay oblivious of the fact that we look for the self, and that is all

I say hello to you as if you are distant

Like you won't know where I am when you hear this

As if you're not the one hearing

But just like this you must not live in reference

Otherwise all meaning is lost, Blue is not red and it doesn't try to be, you are not found in all you try and see

So relax, stop the search

Hello, From now

Section Three:

Passion and
MOTIVATION

How can you ever reach a goal you don't believe is there?
If you keep your dreams in your head, how will they get
into reality?

The problem isn't our lack of desire; it is our lack of
awareness of both the world–its possibilities and our unique
role within it. Discipline? Consistency? Achievement? All
of which are at your disposal as soon as you give them to
yourself, intentionally.

THE GREATEST MOTIVATION IS NOT HAVING ANY

If we wait on life to happen, it will most definitely pass us by. If we wait for ourselves to be found, then we will always be in search of what is already here. At times we overcomplicate life's simplicity with our own complexity. As if we need so much in order to be so little. This is to say that we must realize that anything we desire is only a fraction of who we are—and anything we possess is not as valuable as possessing ourselves. Saying that the greatest motivation is not having any, is to say there exists so much within the world we inhabit. Often people wait to find something to drive them, or to find something that makes their experience worthwhile. When their "worth", would be found as soon as they realize, that they are the very thing that they are looking for. There is no greater reason to do anything, than to do it for those you love, yourself included. When we let down our ego about ourselves and quit expecting the world to treat us with a certain grace, we will begin to treat ourselves with it. The love we experience in life, is in part about the love we have for ourselves. At least to the extent of placing ourselves in the direction of that which loves us, and that which we love. We are always going to be the catalyst for our own change and development. Our growth is based on the choices we make within, that impact all that is without. If we fail to go within ourselves to decide what it is we want, then nothing will ever motivate you to create it. We strive for nothing and nothing is what we will get. We strive for outcome and outcome we may receive. However, when we don't place ourselves at the foundation of who we are, then all we achieve will only be in reference to the external ideas we chase after, typically greater than the current ideas which govern our identity.

To not have a motivation, is to have a blank canvas upon which to decide what you will be motivated by. We must at the very least do things for ourselves—not in a selfish way but in a selfless way. Not being so preoccupied with our perception, that we fail to take steps towards our desires. There is no greater success in life than the abandonment of the idea that you cannot fail. To fail is to try, and to try is to realize that you lose nothing in trying but *gain everything in success.*

YOU CAN'T SEE UP WHILE LOOKING DOWN

You cannot heal what you do not acknowledge. You cannot solve internal problems with external solutions. The negative aspects of life are not to be ignored; *they are to be seen in full.* Granted a perspective which allows them to be a part of the whole of who you are. When we have aspirations to solve these circumstances, we must at first fix ourselves to what we want, not what we want to leave behind. If we are not mindful of the steps we take, we risk going in the wrong direction. If we are only focused on what we want to leave behind, we will never discover the things we have yet to desire. Our narrow focus on what was, closes our minds to what is, and what could be. This is all to say that we need to look towards the present moment more than what's behind us. Not to say don't care for the past or what has occurred within it. Instead, recognize that we still have more experiences ahead to define our lives. Moreso, we have an opportunity to look at what is, and create what we desire, so long as we are present enough to do so.

To say, "You can't see up while looking down", is to say that our focus on the negative does not breed positivity. If we are to develop in a way we can favor, we must feed ourselves good things. This is not directly in a physical sense of the word, rather a mental one. If we only consume negativity from the world, then all we will be able to create is more negativity. The most troubling part of this is not the negativity present within the world. It is the negativity that we feed ourselves that poses the problem. We at a time are both physician and patient, for we are the ones who both cause and cure our ailments. Many of us think we are the illness, when really, we are the cure. Our perspective of ourselves is a direct influence on our perspective of the world. The more grounded we are in our own positivity, the more our vision will be attuned to the positivity ever present within the world around us. Even when there are times of prominent negativity, we will find that inside of each of us resides a love without condition. *So long as we supply it to ourselves without condition.*

Looking down is not just a way of seeing, but a way of action. At times, we undo ourselves with what we do, both consciously and unconsciously. If we never take the time to step forward from the mind, we will never see how unbefitting our actions, and thoughts, are to ourselves. To look up in this way is to renovate your old habits, ones that have brought you down and make yourself new along with them.

Forward Movement

On the path of growth, we must at first experience what it means to be stuck. This stuckness is something that most people experience whether they are conscious of it or not. The comfort of being in the same place, both mentally and physically, creates more apparent "peace" than it should. In my own experience, assimilation with the false assumptions placed upon me was at once a comfort. Allowing low expectations to guide the way in which we traverse through life. From this viewpoint, what we need to do becomes buried in what we expect from ourselves. In living with a low standard, we attract things of low value, not in material, but in who we are.

No person who has ever lived in truth knows everything about themselves. For they have yet to encounter things that bring forth new reactions, or parts of themselves to become aware of. The constant accumulation of new experiences allows for our "self", to deviate from its mental standard. What we do is experience a few "identifying" events and allow those few reactions to guide our self-image. We know the self in these situations, so as a result, we decide to remain where we are known. The notion that who we are is final is the root of a great deal of suffering.

Profound Pondering

We are stuck not only because it's comfortable, but *because we suppress the parts of ourselves that seek out change*. Many doubts are also taken too seriously, especially in the sense that we treat the assumptions about the future as if they are absolute truth. Allowing all the experiences that we have been gifted with in this life, to be treated as nothing. Which in turn makes the present a cloud of anxiety, undoubtedly caused by the expectation that things will not be as we desire. The most alarming detail of all of this is, we are not fully aware of what might happen in the future. With all things that could stress us about the future, if they are to occur, they will, so what is the point of zealous worry? We limit our ability to exist in a peaceful present, because all we live in, is the worry characteristic of the mind. We must simply exist and push on, as life displays the story for us to watch, not for us to predict.

So, if we don't know what's yet to come in the world, how can there be an expectation for us to choose a path?

At times we lack the self-awareness to even know what our favorite food is, let alone what path we want to choose. Society makes us stuck by forcing us to make decisions about a time that has yet to come. We do not allow for trial and error, *for the lack of trial is the error*. Not to say we should not plan ahead, rather that our plans should be in reference to present capabilities, not future possibilities.

If we are stuck, how can we move forward?

     The only way to break the cycle is to be outside of it. We spend our lives attempting to become individuals in a place where many of our choices are made for us. Not many have done something new, without reference to something already in existence. In the game of life, referencing is something that occurs naturally, you see something you like, adapt it to your own use, express it, and allow others to do the same.

Winning the race

    Step brought forth from the countless separate existences converge upon what is considered to be you. We are not but the culmination of the past and the future all at once. To be part of life is privilege, however, to get a head start is to be privileged. From the moment of our fruition, we are taxed, our existence and participation in the race doesn't come free. To be born into a world, at any cost, is in a real sense misguided. We have not the ability to take back what was once given, for it serves us no purpose. This being said there is no purpose in giving up, so the proper implication is to run in a direction regardless of its destination. Run until you see what lies ahead, it is there you will have the choice to change direction. However, we must choose our own, for if the path is too visible then we are on the path of another. A blind jump into the unknown is a great risk to the self, but the only way to emerge affirmed.

"For he who jumps owns no explanation to those who sit and watch"[5] - Jean-Luc Godard

    So, on how to win the race, one must first come to the realization that you are the sole competitor. You create the end goal, as well as the pace of this race. It's our own ordeal, and it can be faced because that's what we are doing all the time. It is the thought of obstacles that creates them, it is he who believes that he has enemies that is one.

it's not about winning the race so much as it is being done with the race itself. The day you win the race is the day that you stop racing. The moment we allow ourselves to live outside of reference to others we awaken to our own experience. When it comes to our goals and aspirations, they are achieved in our ability to not allow the world around us diminish our goal. Keeping an elevated feeling about what we wish to have, so in some way we already have it.

IF

We would only relax the mind we would be able to relax our hearts,

It is because we try to see that we lack sight,

Clouded and incomplete because the thing viewing it is incomplete itself,

Be free in both perception and application

Casting your own flame

To hold your flame in hand, is to confirm that you are the thinker and pilot to your own ship. We hold our flame in our hands yet are only burned if we let that flame diminish. The lives we live lack what is considered to be purpose, for this reason we must find our own. In the countless feats of man, those who possess it find themselves being able to spread their own passions to the masses. To have a flame is not a matter of freedom, rather a reiteration of all that is self. The shackles of the mind are just that, in the mind. All of us are prisoners but not all of us are locked in; we flames who believe we are un-lit diminish our own potential. To have self-belief is to add fuel to yourself, it is the negative mind that makes a negative world. Not to say the mind is not important, or that things aren't inherently negative. Rather, we must realize the mind is what we are not, the body feels, and that much is true. But these are senses, perceptions, something that needs to be processed, and it is my own belief that our mind is the same. We are not our thoughts, we are the thing that is watching them. To realize we are the pilot of the ship is one statement, but the true person realizes how much we engage autopilot. We too often allow our past to impact our perception of the future. To be in control is to be the flame and not the thing being burnt out.

BEING AFRAID

Fear, Anxiety, and Worry are all justifiable reasons for the absence of action. We don't act when we feel fear because the outcome is often uncertain, but to be within uncertainty is to be alive. Life is uncertain, to believe you are even *you*, is uncertain. We do not know what is not knowable, we only work with pieces of our puzzles. However, what we can piece together is valuable nonetheless. The value in something like this is always attained without knowing all about the valuable thing. We can love without fully knowing other people fully, for we do not fully know ourselves, yet love should be present. Anxiety on the other hand isn't discomfort with uncertainty, it's feeling certain that discomfort will occur, causing early suffering. Having an image of what you think may happen, as well as assuming how change will occur. Anxiousness is both chemical and mental. Are these even different? I think the reaction is a chemical response which can be greatly impacted depending on our mental fortitude. We are like our predecessors in that we seek issues to solve them. The only issue with this is often our problems stem from our internal narratives, rather than external issues.

To deal with internal dilemmas, it's important to take a look at reality with an unanalytical eye. At some points, we trap ourselves as the observer, causing us to experience the world through a lens of our past expectations of what the self is. Far deeper than we can imagine, and yet, more visible than an oil spill atop water, the self is all we see and more. We are like the person controlling a watched person.

Somewhere in the back of the mind, worry is similar to fear. Similar in the way that we are uncertain, but also similar to anxiety in the sense that we think we know some truth.

We misaddress the cause of the suffering that sits in front of us. It's like having a fear of heights, but it's the ground that kills you. It's our anxiety that makes the situation bad at most times, for many situations are only negative relative to our own ability, not the nature of our situations.

Between efforts

If we could have all of our solutions

Then why favor answers

Word without action connote them

Which is to say act

And according to action

Not thought

Too much is lost in our effort to experience in mind

What awaits in the world

So have the picture

And experience the image where you are

BE CAREFUL WHAT YOU CONSUME

What causes us pain and suffering? What makes the lives we live worse than they actually are? We are but sponges to the external world. The natural condition of our mind is to be on the cusp of learning new information. When we don't allow our minds to be open in a general sense, we tend to feed ourselves familiar concoctions. At times I feel as though we confuse mental protection with refusal to learn. It's when we allow ourselves to consume that which we know is negative for us, that truly has negative implications. In our misaddress, we add fuel to the fire of our delusions through over thought and mental effort. Instead of focusing our energy on our own forward movement, and in letting things go. We too often project our expectations upon a world full of individuals, who are free to have their own set of expectations. "We are contenders, but we are not always at the center". That is to say that you are important, you are part of this vast world, however, the expectation of focal pointedness is ultimately unrealistic. This absurd egoism can be both a result of high and low esteem and self-image. The desire to be the focal point is a society embedded mindset, it's as if we are taught to base much of who we are in comparison. *It's as if the fact that we are different causes the self to look at others, as if they are the same as us.* We live in a world full of false comparisons, which in many ways get rid of comfortable individuality. There is no room for comparison. All you can

99

ever be is yourself, and those with separate lives were dealt different hands, it's about realizing that space you take up, and playing your cards to the best of your ability. For our ability is not always governed by what we are dealt, but how we use each card.

IT'S BECAUSE THINGS ARE DIFFICULT THAT WE DARE NOT VENTURE

What stops us from pushing towards our goals? Is what we do only governed by what we lack? Or more so what we fear? Often in life we fail to venture into the unknown, as many of the benefits are not served directly to us. Must the reward always be shown before the task has begun? We sow seeds before the fruit is produced, yet we are aware of the nature of the seeds, but not the nature of ourselves? Are we not just as inclined to grow? It is not because we don't know that makes it unattainable, it's because we don't try to understand. *"It's not because things are difficult that we dare not venture, it's that we dare not venture that things are difficult"[6]-Seneca*. We lose much of the day, in expectation of the night. The paths we fail to explore will not harm us; however, the benefit is lost as well. Just as those who play in the lottery lose something at first, they open the door to much more. To task oneself to a journey, is to allow for the possibility of failure. To open oneself to light, you must accept the darkness cast by your illuminated path. In my experience, the difficulty in producing what I think others would like, was not in finding the things they like, rather figuring out the parts of the self I like best to express. When stretching and expanding oneself, a stable foundation is necessary. *The fear we experience is from the absence of action*, just as when you are truly within the act of doing, it starts to lose form as if the task itself is the one doing you. Just as one can only stress while hyper fixated on some action or set of actions. To venture is to accept all possibilities. The willingness to just be as you are, allows you to be the subject to your own change.

This life is not so much a test, as it is an opportunity to witness the beauty in all things, and beauty differs in each person's perspective. So, the task is our own, to be worried about failure is unrealistic when you desire your own success. The aim is to acknowledge possibility and embrace your own potential. To fail in our society in some ways is to not be accepted, but who provides these persons dominion over who you are? What you do and how you wish to express yourself. These parts of you are not to be connoted by those who lack the patience to see who you really are. So, allow yourself to make mistakes and live life, but ensure they are mistakes, not ignorance and stagnation.

Success

To expand upon what is known as success, one must first dissect what it means to be successful. For starters, as people we have stark definitions for what we know as success. However, we are negligent of the root of our definition. To be successful in the eyes of society is to in part relinquish the idea that we can be authentic individuals. To assimilate oneself to an ideal without the proper understanding, is to give up your responsibility to yourself. The moment we let others give us a definition of our own desires, is the second we lose our individuality, our voice. We no longer have what it takes to be ourselves. Forced unity is not a great thing in this sense. We force people to make decisions that they would not make naturally, for the sake of a synthesized society. Success presides over the sects of man able to distinguish self-desire from society, and have them, if necessary, work in conjunction. We can never truly have success negligent of society, steps need to be taken outside the self to see what impacts how we view our aspirations.

The sick man within each of us causes us to think we are lower than others. The part of us that believes that we exist as a reference point, rather than a point of reference. It is because of such comparisons that we are unable to have a genuinely pure sense of identity. The structure of society affirms our identity, it traps us in our own mind and convinces us that we are the thought itself. Thoughts are power, to observe without judgment allows the free person the ability to decipher the discord of life. To be successful is to be genuine to yourself. It is the lowering of expectations that affirms that they exist, to be genuinely successful is to find the passion for the momentous journey. To regale oneself with all that is, without connotation. Allowing what brings you joy, to do just that, and striving to find all parts of yourself that affirm who you are.

Profound Pondering

The impact of negative self thought

In many ways we are victims to our thoughts.
Often, we allow our mind to dominate our perspective of
the world, and our perspective of ourselves. Who we are is
governed by how we think ourselves to be. You think
yourself stuck, you become stuck. The mind is so powerful
if you think it's powerless, it becomes powerless. My
curiosity comes from how malleable the mind tends to be
when it comes to our view. How can you look into the
mirror one day, and decide you're beautiful, then the next
day ugly, when we look upon the same thing. It is said that
how you view yourself is how you view the world. If we
allow our minds to constantly change our perspective of the
world, then we allow it to change our perspective of
ourselves. I find much importance in figuring out how you
feel about yourself and guiding that feeling with intention.
As long as you are able to accept where you are and who
you are, negative self thought has no place. If you set your
foundation within yourself, then you will never need events
in the world to show you your value. You are valuable,
everyone has a great potential for life, which can only be
gained once we stop questioning our ability, and find out. I
have found myself trapped in thought, as many of us have,
about things I have yet to even attempt. I think it's the very
notion of an "attempt" which makes it personal to our
character. It's the way we attach ourselves to certain
outcomes that creates a false sense of self. The way we

separate ourselves from our own success makes it seem out of reach. *Who you are is not governed by what you achieve or possess, but how much of yourself is in your possession.*

While acknowledging the negative is at times a good thing, it's important to not live in your mind's negativity. The mind is a tool we use not always a guidepost for all action, make sure you're willing to give up the things that make you sick. Many times, this sickness is created by our allowance of both doubt and negativity within ourselves. If we are to achieve anything, we must at first think that we can. For "he who says he can, and he who says he can't are both correct"- Confucius. Know that if anything, you should have yourself in your care. Be mindful of what you feed your mind, for it becomes what you think yourself to be, and what you think is in part what you are.

Profound Pondering

Sharpen your defenses

Do not attack the world, but guard the self. Not to protect the ego but to defend from it. For if the ego attacks

It will be hit

It's been too long I think we should split

A self will always be hard to find

If it's the only thing we hide behind

If we were to be

The we could see what's ahead

You cannot reach heaven unless "you" are dead

The miracle comes if you wish it be granted

Especially if in minds certainty it's unslanted

Straight as an arrow

When the shooter is absent

It will fly like a sparrow

If you are just present

IT'S NOT ABOUT FINDING YOURSELF, IT'S ABOUT REALIZING YOU'RE ALREADY HERE

Often efforts to find ourselves lead to the very undoing which makes us think that we need to be "found". It's almost as if by thinking there is a cure, we force ourselves to think that we are sick. However, these ailments are not created by you, so much as they are a product of your absence. It's the relative neglect of what is in front of us that leaves us with what has passed. If all we do is live in the past, we won't have a future to genuinely get to. I realize most of all that you have to be present in order to build your future. There is no past self to overcome and no future self to achieve; especially when the only thing we reference in those moments i.e. the self, only exists in the present moment. All we are and all we will be is right here and now. Not to say we don't change, rather we only build upon the foundation that is, us. The self I find is not a relationship to the world, but a relationship with who you think you are. We spend more time trying to align the idea of ourselves with the world, than aligning our actual self to our idea. We are not stuck in anything but our belief in our stuckness. *Who am I? What's the point of a verbal answer when who we are is much easier expressed than said.* In our effort to find, we lose, however in our effort to see, we become aware; not only of the self but all that our expression contains. How we want to be externally, and how to best care for that which is inside of us. As what is inside is as infinite as we allow, our power is not in what we hold, but what we have. Most of all, our cage is not what contains us, but all we contain within ourselves. We need to make sure to leave enough space for all we are and all we have yet to become. It's not about finding yourself, it's about realizing you're already here.

FREEDOM IS SOMETHING YOU GIVE YOURSELF

When it comes to developing and understanding who we are, we must at first give ourselves the freedom to be expressed. Expression of ourselves to the world, at times, seems like something that comes naturally. However, expression to ourselves is different. I find that self-expression is something that, in part, must be done with intention or awareness. If we aren't present enough to listen, then we won't be present enough to learn. In realizing that everyone has a complex life, we must know we have our own, and that too, must be explored. When we give ourselves the audience we desire from the world, we no longer need to perform. Life once again becomes something that we live, rather than something we think about. Instead of always being in reference, we are allowed to be the subject. In saying that, our cage is not what contains us, *but what we contain within ourselves*; I realize that if our cage is within, then so is our freedom. Being conscious of what we carry is the only way to shed the weight that chains us to our negativity. I think that in an effort to shed our weight, we succumb to it, because we think it takes effort, when it really takes presence. At times being aware of a part of yourself that's seeking out change allows it to do so. Giving ourselves the presence to see what governs us, provides us with the choice to govern ourselves. In a way, to perceive something is to recognize its separateness from you. When it comes to our negativity, if we can see it, then we know it isn't us, as we are the ones perceiving it. So, in a way, *the only way to give yourself freedom, is to recognize where you're being held captive within yourself.*

WHAT YOU TRY TO CONTROL, CONTROLS YOU

In our effort to take possession of anything, we allow it to take possession of us. In the same way that we try so hard to gain "valuable" material, without realizing how our value becomes determined by it. Whatever we invest our energy into becomes part of who we are, so long as our expectations and feelings are dependent on that something. If you want someone to act a certain way, and they don't, then you feel the repercussions. Not to say that everyone's actions are acceptable, rather you must accept people as they are and as they come. As a matter of fact, I think it is important to not force anything in a subtle sense. The more we try to control anything, it controls us. This is to say that our need for control of certain circumstances, is in a way to say that our comfort with ourselves is dependent on how it is. When who we are is dependent on everything outside of us, then who we are is more for how it's seen, than how it is. If you don't go within, you go without, if we neglect our comfort within, we will never have comfort outside. The world around us is not for us to control, rather something that we can influence. The greatest way to influence is to be present enough to see things as they are. In this way, we can see the ways in which we can use what we have, to do what we can. This occurs once we take a step back from our mind, long enough to see the world instead of our mind. When we can't control ourselves, we attempt to control everything around

112

us. When we can't accept ourselves, we have greater trouble accepting the world.

When I say acceptance, I do not mean to allude to liking or favoring how things are. It's about being present enough with them, to see more than just your feelings about them. In doing this, our energy can be more focused on how to solve the problem ahead of us, rather than trying to fix how we feel about the problem itself. We should learn how to attack the problem, more than we attack ourselves by having the problem in the first place. When we contribute to our own negativity, then all we will be able to experience is said negativity. This is not in any way to say feelings are not valid, not in the slightest. It is to say that how we feel takes place in our mind, and action takes place in the world. How you feel about any given thing should act as a catalyst to our action, not a hindrance. To act in a way that we find befitting of ourselves, we will need to take that step back from our mind. Being present enough to see the ways at which we can influence what is in front of us and more so ourselves.

GIVE YOURSELF A CHANCE

How often do you give yourself the support necessary to actually pursue what you want? When will we realize that we are always sufficient for ourselves? The presence that you are able to give yourself is an opportunity to experience who and what you are. If we don't reward ourselves with our own conscious attention, then we will at times act without ourselves in mind. I find that when we do things with ourselves in mind, we grant ourselves an audience. Conscious intention sufficient enough to realize how we are impacted by the world, and how we are impacted by our perspective of it. Realizing the negative impacts of our own actions, allows us to navigate ourselves enough to influence ourselves. Recognizing how you contribute to your life also displays how you contribute to yourself.

The greatest thing you can ever give yourself is not a physical something, rather a chance. A chance to be seen, or a chance to be heard, validated, loved, and so on. I find that at times the very possibility of good can be seen as a good thing. Having some sort of gratitude for who you are, is something I know assists in finding comfort in the world. Giving yourself permission to enjoy the space you occupy and realizing that you are subject to all that you feel. In a way, being grateful for what is currently here, is akin to giving yourself a better outlook, and in essence, a better life. Showing appreciation for what you have is what allows you to gain more.

How can we expect to appreciate what we have yet to obtain, when we cannot appreciate what we currently have. In most cases what we have now are the very things that we wanted in the past. If we can't recognize that our gratitude's should not live in reference to each other, then we will only find our value in what we lack. And the troublesome thing about this, is if you end up possessing what you currently lack, there will be no value in it.

KEEP GOING

The hardest thing to do is the easiest once done. For if we only live in the mind's connotation of what is, *then all we go against is ourselves*. To keep going is to give yourself a better understanding, one which allows you to see things the way they are, rather than the way you are. Then you will know when your mind seeps into the world around you, stopping you from progress. When our world becomes our mind, our mind does not become the world. That in it of itself would be backwards. All that is, is not our mind, for our mind is only part of what we are. So, when we walk out into the world, it's important to know how we create what we experience to a personal extent. This being said, if we stay within the connotation of our mind, then we too, will only be part of ourselves. There is always so much more to be seen and experienced, one of the greatest things being yourself. So keep going, not until you're tired, or exhausted, fatigued, etc. Until you're brought back to life by the very thing that dampens your idea, *you*. I think we must learn how to place within ourselves, what we wish to attain from the world around us. We want certain things because we value them, and we think that by possessing them, we too will have value. What I realize is, *if you are the one who places the value, then you must be more valuable than that which you wish to possess*. This is not to say have no desire, just recognize when what you desire is a representation of what you lack within. There is no path without you, in many ways you are the path that you walk. *If you have any care for your path, or care for what you want to have in the future; Make sure to take care of that which allows you to walk the path in the first place.*

To keep going, is to recognize that regardless of what hardships you've endeavored in the past, you are still present. That in itself deserves affirmation, for you are much stronger than you may allow yourself to believe in thought. The affirmation of circumstances is far less important than the affirmation of self. The love you place within yourself is the love you experience in the world, because you too are a part of the world.

If we can recognize that we are subject to our experience, and our experience is subject to perspective. Then we must, at a time, realize we are truly subject to our own perspective, both of the world and ourselves. Our continued efforts in our endeavor should not be treated as efforts, rather, opportunities. Opportunities for better understanding of who we are, so we can better understand what we are not, the mind.

IT'S ABOUT HOW YOU SEE YOURSELF, NOT HOW YOU'RE SEEN

Our preoccupation with our perception only hints at our inability to decide for ourselves, how we are. This of course is not to say be negligent of all around you. Rather, recognize the way in which we invest trust everywhere, but within ourselves. A certain degree of honesty must of course be present with this, as I feel as though when you learn how to see the good in yourself, you begin to alter the bad. Any overzealous focus on any aspect of one's nature will lead to your undoing by making a negative part the whole of your being. In other words, allowing a singular aspect of yourself to be the most defining part of who you are, when you are much more. Learning to vest love within your perspective of yourself allows you to once again be a person. Instead of a project that must be worked on. It's almost as if the focus stops being against yourself and begins to work in accordance to how you want to be. How we feel about ourselves is ultimately reflected in how we express ourselves, and in how we are perceived by others around us. This is not to say "just neglect others" and say to yourself that "you are a good person" just because you think so. Instead, it's about being present enough with yourself, to feel good about the change you wish to make within yourself, and in your expression to both the world and yourself. To be aware of yourself, is to know how you impact everything that you come in contact with. We, at

118

times, get lost within our acts and forget we are the one who is acting. In the performance of life, the greatest people are the ones who are able to give themselves an audience enough to be as they wish. Grant themselves a perspective which allows their growth, rather than just stagnation.

It's about how you see yourself truly, more so, about how you feel about what you see. If what you can view is something that you don't find appealing. Then the objective is to begin at once, and do what makes you feel best. Give the care to yourself you wish to feel from your experience. If you want to experience the good, begin to create it. If you want to be better, make the choices that lead to your best good. *The point of our introspection is not to find beauty within ourselves, but beauty within what we experience, one of the things being ourselves.*

Passion and MOTIVATION

Section Four:

LOVE

If you don't love yourself, what is stopping you? And why is that something worth depriving yourself of love? How can you give something you don't have?

If we never learn to love the subject of our experience, then it will only be experienced through others and the world. This is to say that when we don't vest love within, then we will only search outside, to no avail.

AS LONG AS YOU HAVE YOURSELF, YOU HAVE SOMEONE

When you only live in reference to everything around you, you cease to be the subject of your own experience. This is not to say pay no mind to the world around you—rather recognize that you too are a part of the world you see. We often look for our missing parts in what we see around us, without realizing that we can give ourselves some of what we lack. This is why I feel it's important to intentionally treat yourself like a friend. When you realize that you spend 100% of your time with yourself, then one might find a subtle importance in appreciating yourself for being there. You have endured all of your life's hardships and are still here to experience more. The importance of this is not to say that more negativity is coming into your life, but to say that you can always be there for yourself. As long *as you have yourself, you have someone*. We need to be there for us. If we are the ones who can see our internal workings, then we must be the ones to validate our internal work; otherwise, we will always be searching for external solutions to internal problems. I find that some of the discomfort in being where we are, is not liking who we are with. It is not the path that needs affirmation, it's the self. When we don't recognize that we need the same care and affection from ourselves, as we expect from the world, then we will only live in reference to the world's ability to keep us afloat. However,

122

the world is not there to help us be who we are. For who we are is already here, just waiting for us to become more aware.

When we give validation to who we are, we open ourselves to greater understanding, as well as a greater opportunity to aid ourselves in our paths. When you walk the path alone, it can easily seem lonely, but you have to realize that there is no path without you in it. So if you cannot affirm the one that's walking it, there's no point in walking it at all. At times affirmation of the self may seem difficult, but there should be no condition to love yourself. The love you have for anything in this world is only possible because you are in the world yourself. This is to say that you must learn to *appreciate yourself for all you appreciate, love yourself for all you love.* Value yourself for all that you find valuable, because at the end of the day, something with no value cannot determine the value of something else. So if you can see anything of value in the world, recognize that you too must have value akin to or greater than what you see.

SELF LOVE HAS NO CONDITION

If we only love ourselves relative to what we do, then we will never love ourselves fully. To have real love for anything is to accept it for what it is, not what it does. I think that the love we give to ourselves is represented in our view of the world we live in. For if we walk in this world without the love we alone can give, we will search for it everywhere but where it resides. This is not to say that love in an external sense is unreal or shouldn't be looked upon. At times when we don't have love for ourselves, we live life thinking it's only about our relation to others. In positing our love and value outside of ourselves, we become dependent on the external, in order to find internal comfort. To say self-love has no condition, is to say that the love you can provide yourself, can be for the sake of your existence. When someone is asked who they are, they are likely to begin listing a set of things they do. We tend to find more value in ourselves in terms of application, rather than embodiment. Having our value in what we see alone is, in some ways, the root of our issue. If we can't learn to appreciate who we are regardless of what we do, then who we are will only be as valuable as we are useful to others. When we live in reference to that utility, then we lose our ability to be authentic to ourselves and others.

Profound Pondering

If we live for a set reaction or outcome, then we are not being ourselves, we are being someone we think can get that reaction. This at face value is not bad. This said, if we were to bring our true self forward, we would be able to see exactly what needs to be changed for our comfort. Many times, this change is not much more than a change in our perspective. Again, this is not to say that we shouldn't have any regard for others, or regard for the world we live in when expressing ourselves. This being said, if we don't allow ourselves to be who we are, then our expression will not be so much ours, as it is a product of our thoughts. If we want to change ourselves in a genuine way, the importance is understanding who you are. If who we are is more easily expressed than it is thought, then we must pay attention. We have to learn to be true to ourselves, then begin to grow. We must begin to do things for what they do to us inside, rather than what they do for us outside. *Otherwise, our love for both others and for ourselves will be as conditioned as we are rehearsed.* In saying this, I mean that love in any real sense, prior to the word, is acceptance of what you are and what something is. When affirmation is done from a standpoint of acceptance, it provokes a greater opportunity to grow into something we can learn to love more. Instead of something we think is lovable.

WHEN WE ARE TIRED WE ARE ATTACKED BY THINGS WE CONQUERED LONG AGO

When are past grievances truly overcome? Is there a point at which we are able to acknowledge the passage of time? More so, how can we determine if we are healed from our smaller grievances? This should be prefaced by saying that there are many things that need much more attention to overcome. What I speak about is mainly in reference to general life and issues constructed by the mind, even those tied to real events. Opposed to physical issues that may be unrelated to our mind's stagnation. The modern healing culture creates a dichotomy between parts of yourself. For the sake of healing or short-term gratification, we separate our issues from ourselves as if they are not a part of who we are. More so, we allow the thought to be neglected to the point of true ignorance. We hide from these parts of ourselves, until we realize they've found us. Waiting until we are found, while easy, leaves us open and exposed to the true negative artifacts of the past. The past is a funny thing; it shows us only part of the story at which a single perspective presides. It's as if only negativity can be reflected and not as open as it occurred in reality. The realities of the present, in a way, have become the delusion of the future. Meaning that the longer we delude our present, the more the future is likely to follow suit. I think our self-care also plays a major role in the accumulation of mental fortitude. It is through our affirmation of self, that

126

we are given a chance to become people who can reject the very things that make us sick.

What we fail to give to ourselves we seek in others. "When we are tired, we are attacked by things we conquered long ago"[4]. We shun our pasts and neglect the power within the present. I think part of this comes from fear, "But he that dares not grasp the thorn should never crave the rose"[7]. In other words, If we want to learn to love who we are we must do so in full. If we seek to find comfort within who we are, we must learn to be intimate with the aspects we intend on leaving behind. Not for the sake of holding on, but for the acknowledgement of letting go. We must accept things as they are and where they are, for all that is, is now. The present is all that is, the past is merely a memory of the present pushed back for the sake of memory. We must strive for balance within the self, grounding the physical, while giving direct attention to our mental. Be aware of yourself and more so the things that guide your image.

Love and happiness

Twisted for right and wrong

They exist in duality

Not that they differ rather,

Those that experience it do

 If we could let our heart feel

Then we wouldn't think about feeling at all

We would feel,

To love is to embrace

To acknowledge

To let go

To be,

And to be happy

Is to love and be aware of it

Profound Pondering

Hallowed by Soft water

We encounter both events and circumstances that move who we are internally, with what seems to be little effort. In my view, we allow ourselves to be hollowed out by soft circumstances, because we have a hard exterior. A lot of us live life with a guard up in order to protect ourselves from the dangers of the modern day. Life can be an experience which presents you with both the good and bad aspects of yourself. Many times, it's our relationship to the circumstance that makes it difficult. Depending on whether or not we make it personal to our character or allow ourselves to be defined by that which is not us. We must be aware of how holding ourselves together implies that we can be taken apart. It's about how you allow yourself to be, without the influence of external events. It is always about how you relate to what you do, and how you contribute to what you know yourself to be. Instead of adapting ourselves to situations, we harden ourselves to try to stop the issue, instead of stopping ourselves from seeing it as an issue.

Many of our issues are so because we find ourselves being attached to the outcome. Whether or not we think we are a reflection of our outcomes, our attachments dictate how our life tends. The importance here isn't to be soft or hard, but to allow your character to exist beyond the standard of your issues. Realize that what you are and what

129

you encounter are not the same, and don't always imply the other. If we are to have any control over the outcomes in our life, the importance is in perspective, not in circumstance. We are only the reaction to our external circumstances, we are not the circumstance itself.

You feel what you feel

To let go of self

Is to embrace feeling

For there is no greater health

Then when head hits ceiling

To bring yourself to air

Is to have you in mind

For if we care

Then we would have the time

DON'T CONTRIBUTE TO YOUR OWN NEGATIVITY

While it can be said that we are not the cause of the negativity we encounter, we at times are the cause of its persistence. Life is often lived in reference to our thoughts about what should, will, and could happen. There is a grand benefit and importance in instantiating presence into our thought process. There is no should or could have, only things that have happened and things we have done. Part of moving forward is leaving the past behind, and our reluctance to let go is what often keeps us holding on. This is not to say don't learn from the past or forget all that has taken place. But, to say that what is not resolved, is bound to repeat itself, so acknowledgement is necessary. In our acknowledgement of the past and present, we tend to live in the negativity that takes place in our experiences. As if what happens around us is in direct reference to who we are and how we should feel, when this is not the case. To say don't contribute to your own negativity is to realize that everything is not here for our direct benefit. However, this does not mean we need to project negativity onto something that we are bound to encounter. In many ways we suffer before it is necessary, by living in our mind instead of the world around us. Even when talking about the self, we have parts that seek our change and things we might even connote as negative. However, *the importance*

LOVE

is not in our connotation, rather in the realization that the less we think we are the cure, the more we will feel sick.

Often our discontent with life is fueled by our constant degradation of self, as well as the experiences we encounter. If things can only be as they are, we must in part be the thing responsible for how we feel about ourselves. This is not at all to say that our feelings are unwarranted, especially when we are talking about morally incorrect happenings and events. With reference to our internal battles, we should stop battling with ourselves. To not contribute to your own negativity is to realize that many of the things we dread doing, are only dreadful in reference. Mainly in reference to other events, people, and places, but they don't exist anywhere but the mind most times. The more we live in our minds, the less we will be able to live in the world. *If we can admit that our feelings can influence our perception; then we should take responsibility for all the beauty we fail to see in the projection of our internal ugliness.*

SHOW UP FOR YOURSELF

We will always be lost, as long as we think we need to be found where we look, instead of where we are. Who we are is in many ways, beyond what we compare to. Part of what creates beauty in our lives, is the fact that it is our lives. Life is fortunately lived only from your view; we alone can view the beauty that is our inner self. If most of who we are is something beyond what can be seen; then we must be the ones to validate that which cannot be perceived by others. To show up for yourself, is to actively participate in the life that you have been given.

The presence that we give to the moment is the moment that we experience. Life is not something we are separate from. *Your life will always feel empty as long as you aren't a part of it.* We spend so much time trying to see life without realizing that life is something we are. The growth of our perspective in and out, is one of the only things that can lead to our salvation. The main thing posing a threat to who we are, is who we think we are. Showing up for yourself is understanding that you are not just your mind, and it's not you vs. you, *it's you and you.* When we allow the wall placed by our identity to dissolve, we realize that much of what limits us, is us. The mind is a powerful tool if you allow it to be a tool, instead of who you are. We are not just the thoughts we have, but the reaction we have to them. In this way, we are separate from that which we

133

hope to escape from. The entire premise of attempting to escape makes chronic implications. We should stress the idea that you shouldn't run from what you want to overcome. If we run from all of our issues, then they have already caught us. I find that it's more worthwhile to be present to confront the issue, *rather than be distant and confront the mind.*

When we place all of our value and energy in what's seen, then we cease to be able to walk our path. As when we aren't present enough to see the steps, we won't know if we are going in the wrong direction. Part of showing up is being present to carry some of the burden we place on ourselves, and intentionally so. When we make the choice to see what is troubling our mind, we establish our separation from that something. Our power is once again our own, instead of being invested in the very things we wish to have power over. When we allow our control to be solely over ourselves, then we allow ourselves the strength to see what is within our influence. That is to say that when we are present with ourselves, we can be present with our opportunities. There is no greater opportunity than choosing to be yourself every day, in every moment. To put yourself into life is to be able to get yourself out of it. In other words when we accept ourselves fully, then everything we encounter will start to be itself, rather than a projection of how we are internally. If we don't validate our internal workings, then we will seek external solutions to our internal problems. *So showing up isn't really about being there to see the world, but being able to see yourself.*

OVERCOMING OVERTHOUGHT

If it's not in your hands it shouldn't be in your mind.
This is not to say don't take action, it is to say that often we
labor ourselves with thoughts about thoughts. In essence
we are fighting fire with fire, as we combat the mind with
the mind. It is not about the effort you place into this
overthought either, it's about letting go of your dependence
on thought. Not to say thinking is unimportant, rather
seeing that the mind is just a representation of our personal
biases. When we feel bad about ourselves, we tend to feel
bad about our world. Which is why I believe that you must
first accept yourself, before you can accept the world. Too
often we allow our mind to be our defining principle, not in
how we think, but in who we think we are. *Who we are is
more easily expressed than it is thought.* I think the
constant effort to define yourself through thought will only
leave you being valued by its bias. We will start to derive
our worth from everything around us, instead of everything
inside of us. In this way, we are no longer the subject of our
life, because we are living in reference to the world. We do
not have to be selfish or narcissistic in any way, we just
have to be where we are. *When we engage in excessive
thought, we lose the ability to think.* This is because our
thoughts are more grounded in our feelings about our
thoughts, than they are in the world. Not to say feeling is
not important, it is, but to say don't contribute to your own
negativity.

Profound Pondering

Overcoming overthought is, in a way, breaking the loop of perpetuated negativity from the mind. Taking a step forward long enough to realize that what we are is not the thought, we are the one observing it. I find that if we commit ourselves to its observation, then we will no longer, for the most part, be dictated by the bias it comes with. Also, Affirmation of the self I feel is important in this battle as well. We have to at a time realize that we are a part of every situation that we encounter. *We don't know what we will encounter however, we do know we will be there to encounter it.* So, if we are present enough to be there when our mind begins to overthink, then we will be able to combat it, not with more thought, *but with more self.*

Journey's end

If I could wait for all time to pass

So I could see what I achieved

Then all I'll see is the result of waiting

It's weird to have sight but lack vision

And to be able to hear without listening

But the only difference is your presence

Vision is awareness of sight

Just as dark is in reference to light

Listening is a remnant of what's heard

Just as limitation is just a word

To lead our journey to an end

We must begin with no intention to end

For the journey is you and yours alone

And if we let it waste, we shall atone

THE PATH CAN'T BE WALKED WITHOUT YOU

If we don't participate in the life that we live, then there won't be a life to be lived. I feel as though life is more often thought about, than it is actually lived. The presence that we give to ourselves is what allows us to be prominent within our lives. The focal pointedness on our path or on our end goals is what I feel contributes to a lack of attainability. *If we are able to realize that the future starts today, then we can realize that our efforts need to be made where we are, not where we are going.* Not saying don't plan for the future, rather plan to build the future in the present. To say the path can't be walked without you, is to present that the focus of our pursuits isn't often for the pursuit, but its relationship to yourself. We often find our value in that which we place value in, and typically that is material and external. However, if we can find value in who we are, regardless of what we do, then everything that we do will be filled with the value we have. This is why I feel like *it's not the path that needs affirmation, it's the self.* Your affirmation of who you are, is what allows you to be who you are. The world is already filled with negativity, especially if you fill yourself with it. If you are able to fill yourself with more positivity, then your world will be filled with more, because you too are a part of the world you live in.

Thought is important; however, it is not the way you are supposed to live in the world. Overzealous thought about the life we live, makes it more thought, than lived. If all you can do is think about it, it is probably not worth thinking about. Not to say that life is not worthwhile, rather it is most beautiful when lived. Life is one of the most beautiful things to experience, especially if you are present for the experience. Our attempt to predict the future, when it comes to our lives, creates expectations that we depend on. The more dependent we are on our expectations, the more we will be dependent on the outcomes. So, the importance isn't to not have any expectation, it's to allow yourself to be comfortable where you are, regardless of what you think will happen.

RENOVATION

If you keep using the same bricks, you'll keep building the same house. The importance here isn't in getting new bricks at all, it's renovating the ones present. Too often we rid ourselves of an opportunity for growth, by getting rid of the parts of ourselves that seek out change. If we're always discarding, then we'll always have vacancies. Life is about filling yourself back up intentionally. I find that we cannot replace bad habits with absence, It will just be once again filled with something that is not our choosing. The positivity we give to ourselves in our pursuit of being built is displayed in our very structure. If we have to constantly compromise our structure, in an effort to get rid of bad parts, then we open ourselves to the risk of collapse. In saying this, it's much more important to be conscious of what we wish to cast out and find a way to make it new.

If I'm impatient and "I" wish to be patient, there is no such thing as just plainly getting rid of my impatience. I must in a way replace it with what I wish to be in its place, otherwise my impatience is likely to return. The intention that we vest into our experience, often allows our lives to be lived, rather than just seen. We spend a lot of our lives waiting for life to happen, without realizing that we are the life that we experience. If we never come to this conclusion, then life will always be more viewed than experienced. If all we do is analyze the life we live, then the only thing that will be experienced is that analysis.

This is why renovation is so important. If we can recognize the parts of ourselves that need change and make them into something good intentionally. We will be one step closer to realizing who we truly are. I find that there is a part of you that remains whenever you change, this part being akin to your soul or being or whatever you want to call it. So, when we do cast out, we often are neglecting parts of ourselves that need attention enough to be renovated.

STOP THINKING START BEING

If all we can do is think about it, then that thought has no place in the world. "A man who thinks all the time has nothing to think of but thoughts"[8]- Alan Watts. I find that the importance of perspective is not to encumber yourself with thoughts, but to find yourself outside of them. It can easily be said that how we think about ourselves, impacts the way we interact with the world and with ourselves. If we only use thought as our defining principle, who we are will always be in reference to what we already know, rather than what could be. If we want to explore our own potential, the importance is to express, not rehearse who we are. Oftentimes, *who we are is more akin to a role being played, rather than a story being written.* It's more important to be as we are, as who we are is more easily expressed, than it is thought about. When we don't allow ourselves to be outside of what we know, then we limit how much we can actually learn about ourselves. At times accepting that you don't know, is the first step to being able to learn. *stop thinking, start being.* If you want to change who you are, you must begin going beyond your current thoughts about yourself. When our mind can't define who we are, we will look towards our actions. If what we embody is akin to the same stagnation that our mind has, then we will never be able to truly change.

143

LOVE

Sometimes we need to act in accordance with what we want, as well as fix our thoughts to better see the opportunities ahead of us. When we live our lives in thought, we often don't get the chance to live in the world. To only live in thought, is to only experience what we think, not the world you live in. Therefore, living in a world of connotation, instead of a world of possibility.

Profound Pondering

Avoiding the rain

I always found it interesting how we shelter from bad weather

How we avoid the rain

It's no question that there exists discomfort

As does all of life

Especially if we don't find comfort within ourselves

There's a beauty unknown to the comfortable

It's when a storm forces nature to dance

Making it all work in accordance to its harmony

You may think nature finds it uncomfortable

But uncomfortable is its nature

Because like us

It is the cause of its "suffering"

YOU FIND YOURSELF IN EVERYTHING

Who am I? What am I doing with my life? What do I like? All of these questions that many of us ask on a regular basis, often offer unsettling or unheard answers. When we open ourselves to these questions, the answer at times is taken from us. It's not that these are not good things to ask, rather, we look for the answer in our mind instead of the world. The question of "who am I?" especially, we too often attempt to define who we are, through our thoughts alone. To the point where acting out of accordance with what we think causes us discomfort. In other words, we need to learn how to genuinely figure out who we are, beyond our thoughts. It can easily be said that our thoughts influence the way that we perceive the world around us. In saying this, I do not hope to allude to an abandonment of thought completely. Rather, saying that if we continue to compound upon who we have been with our thoughts, how can we expect new growth? Especially when who we are is more easily expressed, than it is thought. Should we not focus more on being present to choose our expression? When we live our lives on autopilot, many can attest to the troubled nature of one's expression to themselves. When we allow all of our expressions to be rehearsed. We lose the ability to be authentic to who we actually aim to become. Embracing the unknown aspect of the present moment is something I feel aids in this endeavor. For when we allow ourselves to be fully in the moment void of our own anxious thoughts about how we ought to be, we allow ourselves to be. Within this *being*, I believe we can begin to answer some of our most fundamental questions.

Who am I? Be present enough to see who you are, or at least to see who you have been. Also, giving yourself enough presence to make the proper choices which align with who you wish to become. What am I doing? Sitting there thinking…instead of asking yourself what you should be doing? This question, however, often leads to another, what do I like? The answer is found in our ability to be present with our actions and opinions when we do experience new things. If we aren't present while doing, then our feelings tend to be more of a rehearsal, than a reaction. So, the importance here is to be present with yourself long enough to see how you interact with both the world, and yourself. In this way, you can find yourself in everything.

YOU LOSE YOURSELF BY NOT LETTING IT BE FOUND

When it comes to being a person rather than a project, we have trouble recognizing the change that occurs in our acceptance of how we are. It seems as though as soon as you realize or pay attention to the way you are, you gain possession of the reins. Our perspective is necessary if we are to change and influence ourselves to our liking and understanding. When we keep our eyes closed or hyper fixate on small parts, we lose the beauty within the complete picture. *No more of the self is lost, than in our insistence on not letting it be found.* Many life experiences act as catalysts to our internal experience and vice versa. When we come into the moment heavily encumbered with our ego, we fail to ascend to the height of our possibilities. The notion of the self is something that we too can become preoccupied with. Too much thought about any one thing leaves you thinking of nothing but more thoughts.

The cyclic nature of a mind disengaged with the beauty of the unknown, is likely to repeat things which strip us of our joy. The best part about being yourself is being able to experience it. Us setting wide intentions about who we are is imperative, I believe them to be vital in taking the right steps. However, *if all we do is think about the step itself, when it will actually be taken.* Sometimes it's about being present enough to forget that you are walking a path at times, and just simply enjoying the view around you. Not to say don't be cautious, rather don't be so preoccupied with the chance of failure that you miss your opportunity at success. We experience life more in our own mind than the actual world we think of. Giving yourself grace and having faith in yourself is integral to actually finding yourself in this world. *For if we only think about how we fit in, then when will the fitting actually be done.*

Not to say reject all thoughts about anything relating to yourself. However, it is pushing those of us who tend to be driven by our own introspection, to realize how we are also within everything around us. *Not in a sense of causation, but in a sense of you being the life that you experience.*

DO NOT OUTPACE THE MOMENT

There is nothing but what is. In our efforts to achieve, we often live in the future and disregard what we have in the present. When overzealously focusing on what we lack, we lose everything we stand to gain. If we can never be within the moment we are given, then there will be nothing to enjoy but fleeting moments of achievement. At times, when we allow our value to be vested within the outcomes of the world, we become driven by labels, rather than passions. *A goal without action is just thought.* If all we do is think then it's probably not worth thought at all. We can't get anywhere on our path without taking steps from where we currently are. To say "do not outpace the moment" is to say be so much within what is, that you can actually create what you desire. The moment provides insight and ability to do many things. For in the moment, we can act upon the opportunity that is ourselves. The subtle preoccupation with things to be a certain way, or the expectation that we have of the future, is typically based in fear of the present. In a subtle way, we don't fear the moment, rather we are not content enough with who we are to let ourselves experience it. This is why it is so important to vest some type of love within the self, otherwise our love will be a transaction we gain only through achievement. Instead of something we unconditionally give ourselves on the basis of our very existence. We should of course strive to be better and strive to obtain things that we desire. However, if we can't appreciate what is, then no amount of anything will fulfill us. Our gratitude should not have to live in reference to other gratitude's, in order to be valid.

To be present is to not prefer to be anywhere else. Not in a sense of thinking this is the best it could be, rather recognizing there is no point in degrading where you are in awe of something relatively better. We can and should recognize better things at which to desire. However, we need to learn to not let our desire for future things cloud our appreciation for what we currently have. In focusing on what we lack, we always lose what we currently have, and what we stand to gain by being in the moment. It has been said before, the best way to choose your future, is to be present enough to build it. The best way to be a better person is to be present enough to choose actions and thoughts which align with that idea. If we are never in the moment, then the only thing we outpace is our ability to succeed where we are.

THERE'S STILL MORE TO EXPLORE

If we allow our curiosity to be dampened by the world's familiarity, then we too will be dampened. The more we treat our lives as mundane, the more we will experience a world lacking interest. How we see ourselves is how we see the world in many ways. The more we think that our growth is over, the more our experience will remain as we are. When we allow our gratitude's to live in reference to each other, we lose our ability to truly be in the moment. In the same way, we should focus more on creation than analysis, and we should allow ourselves to continue to see what has yet to come. We live in an unstable perspective when we are stuck in analysis. This takes place when we are stuck in the words and ideas that surround our experience, rather than the experience itself. We are unable to analyze at the same time we are attempting to create something new.

Additionally, if we never move from where we are, we will never see what is left for us.

We all have far greater potential than we give ourselves credit for. Living life intimately means recognizing the importance, is to continue to find things to be affectionate towards. In recognizing that there's still more to explore, we must realize that the exploration always starts internally. If we cannot see past our own issues and hysteria, then we will never experience the

world around us, we will only experience our own
projection.

A large number of us do not wish to live in our
negative prescriptions about the world. We must at some
time realize that we are the ones continuing to take this
nostrum of suffering. *Not to say that we alone are
responsible for what we experience; rather, we at times
have the ability to choose how we experience certain
things.* Feelings at all times should be acknowledged, but
they are not things that need to be lived in. Our rumination
in our negativity only perpetuates it. Our acknowledgement
of the positivity that has yet to come, places us further in
the moment. Being in the moment in this way, gives you
the power to create positivity in your own life. The beauty
of the world is not dampened by the beauty that was
present yesterday. We too are new along with the day, and
our beauty and appreciation should be renewed in turn.

YOU ARE WHAT YOU'VE BEEN WAITING FOR

It is said that if you wait on life to happen, it will pass you by. So, what happens when you wait on yourself? There are many things that we look for to fill the vacancies created by our past perspective. If the way we look at the world is void of ourselves, then we will only be in search of who we are, in things we aren't. We have to understand that the beauty in life is created by the beauty we have within. If we are lacking beauty within, then it is about creating a perspective which allows it to be present. We constantly wait for change without realizing, we can create change ourselves. We wait for support without recognizing we can support ourselves. We wait for love before we believe that we can love ourselves and that we are deserving of love. This is not to say that we should not accept validation from external sources. Rather, we must learn to give to ourselves what the world does not give to us. We will always be lacking when we don't give ourselves all that we already have. This is to say, we must support and acknowledge all of the good that we already carry and begin to carry it with pride and passion. Learn to treat ourselves with enough love, to be disciplined in our thoughts and supportive of who we are.

The main block that we find when trying to work on anything, is our thoughts. When we allow our negative perspective to cloud our view, all we see is reflective of what we lack. We have to be the ones to validate who we are, for we are the ones who know ourselves best. You are with you 100% of the time. There is no beautiful experience you witness, that you aren't a part of. We are always a catalyst for our own experience. If we don't recognize our own participation, we will always think we are a bystander. In playing this sideline role, we neglect to realize we have a part to play in the game. We have a part to play in the lives we live, for life comes from us, not at us. If we don't have a part to play, then there would be nothing for you to experience. And experience is something we all have, so we must begin to experience ourselves, along with what we see. Give ourselves room to be ourselves, as well as room to vest more love into who we are.

Section Five:

Expression

Is a performance good before or after the applause starts?
How do you intend to be heard if you never listen?

We will always be stuck in a performance until we give
ourselves an audience. The freedom of expression isn't a set
thing, and just because it's free doesn't mean it should be
without intent or awareness.

WHY NOT YOU?

To know it is humanly possible, means you too can do it. Oftentimes, we allow our dreams and aspirations to be put on the backburner of our actions. We act as if we know that it is possible, yet don't acknowledge its real attainability in our own lives. *If we don't give our dreams reality, they won't be within it.* Do not give up on what allows you to stay afloat in this world; rather, understand that if you want something, and you know it exists, then it's your job to go out and get it. Even so, many could attest that the major battle within all of this, is the battle within the self. When we think about what it is we want, we often are riddled with thoughts that take us away from our desire. *Do I deserve this? Do I need this?* The better question is: *do you want it?* The value we give to ourselves is what allows us to push towards things of value. "He who thinks he can and he who thinks he cannot are both correct". If our value of ourselves makes us think that we cannot achieve, then it's about changing our perspective to accommodate what we want. In a way, bringing ourselves to the level of our desires, so its value does not make ours seem invalid. When we place what we desire too far above us, it becomes out of reach. It is only once you allow things to be as they are, that you can be as you are, especially in your pursuit of change. This is not to say be stagnant and view what you want as unimportant. *Rather, to view yourself as important and what you want as something you simply want to get, because it's important to you.* When we give ourselves enough presence in our lives, we grant ourselves the vision to see our opportunities. We all have a vast amount of potential unknown to our finite minds. If we don't make attempts to do what has yet to be done, we will only do what already has.

If we never try to succeed, then we will only succeed at not trying. To try is to succeed in this way, when we open ourselves to possibility, we always have a chance. For man cannot predict what has yet to come, but we do know we will be there to experience it so long as we still exist. Saying why not you is saying that even you don't know how much you can achieve, until you try.

Profound Pondering

For those who can hear the music

We at times exist in a state of worry about what has yet to come. Choosing to analyze our lives through the lens of suffering, instead of our love. The meaning contained in life is given to those who live it, not those who just observe it. The philosophical idea of absurdism explains this in part, rather than the standard nihilistic attitude that nothing has meaning, proprietors of absurdism would say this is only partially true. This meaning is given, however with all things that require perspective, these ideas are subject to the biases within the human mind. We must at first rid our minds of this bias to see the picture in full. Half the battle is knowing, the rest lies within ourselves, as we often feign ignorance to avoid life's troubles.

Being indifferent to life seems great, as life seems to contain too much to allow it all to funnel through our minds. Then again, suppressing too much is not helpful to an individual's growth. A quote attributed to Nietzsche, "And those who were seen dancing were thought to be insane but those who could not hear the music". In other words, most people don't know your story, and you don't know theirs. For this reason, we as a society tend to impart unfair judgements upon those who are different from us. We act as if others know what creates our character and defines our happiness. We must at some point stop feeling uncomfortable that others cannot hear the music, and appreciate that we can hear our own.

Profound Pondering

Who will mourn the trees

Life is meant to be let go

So it may be appreciated

Not in the sense we know

We just need it demonstrated

So into the woods we go

Then you decide if you hate it

What stands tall will fall, So appreciate the stand

Especially when life draws

And soon you'll be one with the land

You must listen when you call

Or you won't be manned

Who will mourn the trees

For they must be mourned before they go

If we go unappreciated

Then we will never know

How much we enjoy the self

And reaping what we sow

And appreciate our health

For allowing us to grow

Expression

Sparks of Divinity

To understand that experience is a collective, is to affirm yourself among those who can call themselves conscious. The nature of man is not that of selfishness, rather that of suffering. This suffering is all part of the ordeal that creates the separation between life and death. As if life occurs at the moment of your fruition and death the opposite. Existence, however, has no connotation, it's the implications of life and death that divide our minds. We have so much time yet so little, so we bore ourselves to add more interest to the world. We allocate our energy in part, both to maintain social standing and to preserve a self-identity. To have a spark, as all do, is another way to say we are limited. For this reason, we must choose wisely what our energy is funneled into.

We can be the spark and the charger that allows others to use their own. However, we sometimes charge those who willfully reject assistance only to truly view themselves as the victim. To be a victim at least in everyday, morally consistent situations, is to give up some responsibility. To shock others ignorantly is one way to reject our true design. Compassion and morality can be taught, but for those who reject the teaching, the responsibility is their own. To be responsible for this act is to realize, our voltage is subject to change. The world will continue to advance, and those who reject the change will

162

be but the victims of their own pride. Pride in this sense is neglect, neglect of your own impact, of your voltage, and those who are shocked. We all contain within us a spark, but the utilization of which is not within our egos reach, for when ego dissolves, we cease to be a spark but the whole light.

DILUTION OF THE SELF

As we allow ourselves to take up space, we must acknowledge the space we take up. Given that we have an identity, we must realize how we dilute it by constantly thinking it needs to be fixed. The stress of life, often caused by our own search for stress, is expressed as we seek our issues as our predecessors once sought food and resources. However, we are not always aware of the stress we seek, as many of us are taught to look. In a world where much is given, *we can only focus on what we lack*. The instability that brings us all into being, is also the cause of our end. In life, we are given both mind and body, we grow, change, and develop all unintentionally at first. Everything has value in the eyes of the self-negligent man, even our own degradation.

We seek control, but that very seeking controls us. Control needs power, and in most ways, we are driven by things outside of ourselves. Society is almost so influential it cannot be seen. It could even be argued that part of who we are, is in direct relation to those around us. Would it not be wise to learn from the better parts of great people? For we too are capable, because we too are human. There must be a part of ourselves that is truly genuine, this genuine part of self I feel is invisible, so long as we don't look within. We are like water in a glass. Outside of this glass we are infinite yet undefined. This absence of definition is the allowance of self in full which is eventually diluted by life. *The more we think we are, the less we truly can be.*

It is my idea and many before, that identity should be somewhat of a fluid thing. We should be adaptable, not immovable. Sometimes to heal, we must be something which can acknowledge how it's been harmed, and in this "Being" we must relax ourselves.

EXPECTATIONAL FREEDOM

At times, we commit ourselves to overthinking through the obstacles we face. However, the major issue when we treat the mind with so much power, is that we become subject to the biases that are present within. *The mind is a tool not a counsel.* We cannot wholeheartedly believe what is easily altered by external circumstances, especially if we don't actively impact it ourselves. All that cannot be seen should not *always* be trusted. Interestingly enough, we fail to realize how situations may unfold contrary to our previous thoughts. So, trust in the mind should only be concrete, if and only if, we recognize how it can take us away from ourselves. We tend to generate expectations from a basis of fear and self-protection. We have many hardships we endure in life and few happen outside of the mind. Trust in your ability to endure, instead of worrying about a random outcome formulated from our egos lack of esteem. *Freedom in real life would be to expect nothing and appreciate everything.* I am currently struggling (2022) to differentiate and determine what expectations should be held onto. Like where do we become self-preserving? What is being insecure or selfish? Does this sort of negative outlook stem from instability or is it grounded in truth? I myself do get anxious at times about things that do not make much sense. I think there must be a proper distinction between intuition and anxiety.

Intuition is calm, whereas anxiety is stress caused by direct thoughts in un-based action.

　　If we want to commit to overthinking, we will spend much time trying to accept all outcomes to reach peace. It is only when we allow ourselves to be accepted that true peace comes about. Something that helps is establishing worth in self that is not based on the external world. It is truly a journey where the person must first fill themselves, before they are truly able to give. Give yourself all that you can, in this way, your external environment can be seen clearly. This does not mean to be walked over. You must be open to feeling and allow your environment to stimulate your growth. Be all that you need and be open to receive that which you fail to give yourself in your perspective. *Abundance is in mentality.*

I want to be a song

I want my words to wash over you like song and revitalize your very vessel of its wrongs

To express love not in its subject

But all it references

Expression

A SERIOUS JOKE

Do we take life too seriously? Are the lives we live too stressed? Recently, I've found that there is a profound difference between existence and living. We all exist, but do we take the time to truly live? It's not as if we don't live our lives; rather, we are nothing but passengers to the lives we live. Not to say real living is conscious effort, rather *to live is to be unanalytical of your own existence and instead a creator of it. It is in the mind of the thinker that the self exists, but it is in reality where he lives.* To try without trying, the epitome of the paradox of human consciousness or life. It is almost as if the more we try, the harder life seems. Just as a stressed eye in search, will always find things to stress over. The world is as subject to perspective as we are. So, we must be intent on viewing the world in a certain manner. How can one try not to try? How can one be conscious while being unconscious at the same time? It's like imprinting on your own mind. Becoming so intent on a certain ideal that it becomes part of us, in the way that it impacts our actions without knowing. It's an act of realizing who we are has always been a commitment we make. Even if we feel as though we are not confident, we are confident in that notion. There is no aspect of who we are that has nothing to do with our acceptance and agreement. All we are is the reaction we have to the outside world. If we are able to alter the way at which we react to the world, we can

168

effectively change who we are. *We play the game of life so well we forget we are at play.*

DON'T BE PATIENT, BE PRESENT

In what ways have we betrayed ourselves through our inaction? Life contains countless opportunities, and we at times find ourselves at the very cusp of our desires, *yet we remain still*. Even with all the resources and tools at our disposal we find ourselves stuck. What breeds this stagnation can be attributed to our inability to see ourselves. It is not that we cannot, rather the fact that we think we cannot, that often holds us back. How the world is viewed from your perspective is how your world will tend to be. While easy to say, the implications provide us with a deeper understanding of the most simple things. We often find ourselves at a crossroads between what we know ourselves to be, and how we want ourselves to be. What we know is built over the years, in relations and constant analysis of the world around us. In a sense, what we know the self to be, is just what we have accepted the self to be. We are at times as we think. Which is why it comes as no surprise that what we would like ourselves to be, feels so distant. We tend to treat our past and future as if they do not contain the present. However, the reality of it is that you will be there regardless, and waiting for your own change often bears no fruit. It's you who has to make the choice to change, there is no past to overcome, no future to reach. All you are, is whatever awareness you have now. The present is the only place where we can be, for it is all that is.

Profound Pondering

Patience is not to be forgotten. It must be made present. We wait tirelessly for things to align within ourselves, without realizing that we are responsible. It is you who helps you. It must be you who confronts all those parts of you that seek our change. However, there is no stress to this, you are living for the first time and your story is your own, but make sure you're the one writing it.

FOOLING THE SELF

Often in the lives we live, information we come across in regard to the self is not much but cluttered nonsense. The first self, the birth-given identity, is not created by much but external people and circumstances. The self or the second identity, comes about when people reach a point of acute awareness. For in life there is no self if there is nothing to perceive it. *As sound is just vibration until it hits an ear, we are nothing until we can see ourselves.* We must have some introspection in order to affirm our identities. The space we take up is supposed to be used. As with all things, we must be conscious of how we do so. In our case, I believe it's better to invest in positivity. We all live in our own personal heaven or hell, depending on our view. Righteousness of self is created by sowing love into yourself, realizing that you are your only consistent company.

"The first principle is that you must not fool yourself and you are the easiest person to fool"[9]

-Richard Feynman

What we preoccupy our minds with, oftentimes holds us back. The last thing a person should be, is a victim to themselves or better yet their own perspective. This is why we must be mindful of what impacts us, and mindful of what has created who we think ourselves to be. You have to determine what is pulling your strings, and make the choice to pull your own. Any true definition of self must have you as a primary source. All we have is our internal workings, the parts of ourselves that do not get to bathe in the light of day. So if a certain faulty introspection is making you think less of yourself, without real reference, it must be addressed. Negativity and self-degradation are too easy and too common.

"Talk sense to a fool and he will call you foolish"[10]

-Euripides

And we are the fool. Logic often is displaced by perception and feeling, which in some cases is not negative. However, when feelings are brought by uncertainty and mental insecurity, they have no place in the core of man. We are meant to transcend our ignorance, for it is the only way to shift from being a fool, to being yourself. View all as it is but also acknowledge that you are as you wish to be. And you can be something worth everything.

THE POWER OF SILENCE

It only has to make sense to you. The lives we live should be in reference to ourselves, not all the things we reference ourselves to. Our intentions and desires do not have to be shared with the world, to be expressed within it. The validation we give ourselves should be sufficient and frequent, so we have no need for external validation. Not to say that we can't accept it from the world, rather we should have no expectation for it. The world will provide you with what you need, not always what you want.

We must at times realize that the path we walk is who we are, and waiting for someone to tell you to take a step will only slow you down. Your pace is dictated by you and you alone, which is why it's important to not put on airs about your improvement. There's a certain honesty we must express to ourselves to traverse who we are comfortably. Especially when we want to have our expressions be truly genuine. When you are being truly genuine, no outside perspective will be able to shake you. However, when we fail to see our current truth, then all we will experience is a lie. Not to say what you will encounter is fake; rather, you are closed to yourself.

Who you are isn't something that you hold onto, it's something that you let go of so *you* can remain present. Letting go is what makes it stay, holding on implies that it would escape if we let it. Who we are isn't feeble and it can never leave you. This being said, your mind can take you away from yourself. Our experience in life is, at times, governed by the thoughts and feelings we share for ourselves. If you can't accept where you are, you have no way of knowing how close you are to your aspirations, to yourself. If you don't acknowledge a wound, how can you treat it?

The Space between thought

Our preoccupation with the self leads us to not see others. If our focus is only on our own greatness, we can never see the greatness in all. We must step beyond ourselves to see what is now for us.

YOU ARE NOT YOUR PROBLEMS

I find that in our effort to confront any of our issues we really only confront ourselves. To accept something as a problem is, in a way, to say that part of who you are is invested in expectation. Not to say we shouldn't have problems; rather, we must realize our contribution to our own undoing. The very dependence on external factors to bring internal peace, is the same as looking for external solutions to internal problems. The only place you find yourself is where you are, and the only place peace is found is where you create it. The more we allow ourselves to be separate from our issues and problems, the more power we will have to solve them. What's being solved will be what sits in front of us, rather than what dwells within us. Our projection of our feelings into the world isn't something new. Rather, something we must become aware of. To run from feeling is to run from self, and we can only learn as much as we are willing to listen. This listening to the self is something I think is quite necessary, as we cannot heal what we fail to acknowledge. In saying that we are not our problems, I mean to say that we are only the reaction to them. If we can give our attention to the reaction, then we can see why we have the problem in the first place. Of course, there are blatant issues in the world, but when it comes to ourselves, the issues can be subtle. Instead of addressing our internal problems, we project them onto the things we see outside of us.

Profound Pondering

If you don't go within you go without. I think our main issue isn't inability to see our internal issues, but not giving them the audience to be seen. In giving yourself that space, you open up the door to more understanding of both yourself and whatever you may encounter. It's important to separate yourself from that which is not you, otherwise we become the very problem we hope to solve. *If parts of us are vested in our problems, how can we ever hope to get rid of them without getting rid of parts of ourselves.*

Your whole life

If your life was a moment

Would it be past or future

Unknowing I answer neither

For neither includes what is now

And how to stay here don't ask me how

But I know I have the answer

As long as I have myself

For it is not man but mind

That decides his wealth

Expression

The problem is solved in between

For it is only in the middle where we are seen

A blade of grass could be all of life

And when it points to the sky it also hangs low

For it's only when you take a bow that you know you can grow

A man in his garden

Only can tend to himself

For a life full of self

Is part of your health

Not in avoidance but the unity of authenticity

That will bring this world to an epiphany

Your whole life has been in the present

So why live in the past as a part of a trinity

For only now can I decide what is to be,

Your whole life

Profound Pondering

If you can Gather it in thought, validate it in reality

Why spend so much time in your mind, when all that you desire is in the world? Our effort to find our desires is often done more in our heads than in reality. What we like, what we want, and what we have are all in the present moment. When we are trapped within our minds, we are truly unable to see what surrounds us. If all we can do is think about it, then the thought probably is not worth the time it occupies. *"A person who thinks all the time has nothing to think of but thoughts"[11]*-Alan Watts. That is not to say reject your mind or mental capacity, rather realize what you are is beyond it. All that we hope to have, can only be gained if we take the steps that are in front of us. To gather it in thought is reason enough to pursue it in the world. To know it is humanly possible means you too can do it. What we can achieve, is in part measured by our relative perception of its achievability. Which is why I think the most important thing to validate has always been yourself. If we can recognize that we are the ones that walk our path, then we must give to ourselves as much as we hope to get. Bring yourself in some way to the level of your desire and treat it at times as if you already have it. All great things occur first in mind, as ideas are validated when we take the time to bring them into the world. If we can find a way to give ourselves that validation, then we too will be in the world instead of our minds.

179

Expression

the Future starts today, Not tomorrow

When we allow ourselves to be fully dictated by the idea of time, we are often led astray by our own perceptions. When we allow tomorrow to impact today, then we have already lost our ability to dictate ourselves. Don't lose day in expectation of night. The importance in this practice is to be where you are. The power within the present moment is what creates the future you live in. For the "future" we chase, will just be another present moment. If we look into the future and expect it to be a certain way, void of our current actions, then we are again mistaken. I find that the most beneficial objective is to affirm where you are, so you can get to where you want to be. It's not just about using the present as a means to get to the future. It's about *realizing that the future you are chasing, is in the present moment*. If we don't do what we can with what we have, then we lose everything we stand to gain. Our preoccupation with time has allowed our growth to be dictated by each passing second. When we restrict our understanding of ourselves to this flow, we halt our own. Who we are is gradual, not focal pointed, and I think it's important to recognize that you must choose yourself, over and over. Half of the battle is walking into it, and if we don't take the time to affirm ourselves, we will never reach it. To say the future starts today, is to show that you have to be present to build the future. All great things were at first ideas, and if someone isn't present to validate them in the world, then they will never arrive.

What you put in is what you get out, and if you put yourself into the moment, that's what you will receive. In this same light, if we are to start building our future now, in this present moment—Only then will what we desire be sooner in the moment with us, rather than in our thoughts about the future.

How relative is understanding

If I were to be at the answer

Would I affirm it by asking no questions

Or would I open my mind

To consider what destined

I ask no questions

Yet still I am tested

Should one question the value

Of what they invested

To cash out is to trust the path

Not to withdraw your glove from battle

For it was thrown on the ground

Expression

So wait for the crime
Before you throw down the gavel

You think you can judge
Because you judge what you think
You think yourself a drudge
When man begins to sink
So I begin to question
As man does his art
For he can fail
If "he" never parts

You're closed like a hand does to beg
If he thinks his desires are in his head
Then he's been misled
The best way to steer is to watch the road
And listen to the world for it speaks in code
You against the world
Puts us in toil
When ego is involved, blood begins to boil

A NEGATIVE MIND CREATES A NEGATIVE WORLD

If we can accept that we are subject to our own perspective, we should accept the responsibility we have to ourselves. If we only focus on the negativity within ourselves, all we will be able to see outside is said negativity. I find that when we confront our own flaws, we often treat them as if they are the whole of our being. As if what we see in ourselves is a representation of all we are, when it is not. Who we are is more about our reaction to ourselves, than it is our reaction to the world. *Our life is often defined by how we define ourselves.* If we can't posit any love within who we are, our reaction will be to seek it in all we experience. This is not to say don't seek what is good, rather to say there is always good within and around you.

Certain circumstances of course can strip this view away from us in an external sense. However, if the good you see is within you, then it can never leave, regardless of the circumstance. In this same way, when we only embrace and focus on our negative aspects, we unfortunately bring them into everything we are a part of. Projection in this way is both what we see and what we are, what we experience and how we are experienced. This is why I feel the subtle importance is to be present enough to see how we take away from ourselves. How much joy and love we

183

have denied ourselves in an effort to run from our negativity. *What we run from has already caught us*, and if our focus is on running, when will we take the time to see the good?

In an effort to reject the negativity within us, we perpetuate it and allow it to be in a sense chronic. If we confront that part of us, we would truly realize that it is only a part. In being present with this "part" we can also see the potential we have to change it. Even if it starts small, I think it's important to face yourself and learn to love what you are facing. For if what we think is what we are, then all we have to do is change our thoughts and the world will be new with them.

Failure to fail is not success

If we don't try we will never fail

For to fail is to say you've tried

Given effort to life

And all you've received is yourself

You may think that's nothing

But to the right eye, this is success itself

To realize that you weren't the failure

You were the one who tried

Give yourself to what is

For if you don't, you've lied

Expression

When you are present you build your future

When you allow yourself to be a part of the moment, you are granted an opportunity to influence what is. To say this, is to present you with the idea that your presence is what allows you to succeed. However, it is not presence alone that allows success. When we are present, we can actually see opportunities to gain that which we desire. To create anything, we have to be there to create it. We have to use what we have to create what we want. If we do not grant ourselves asylum from our mind's bias when trying to create, then what is produced will only be representative of the mind's undoing. If we don't take care of ourselves fully, we seek to lose all that we are. To say when you are present you build the future, is to affirm that when you are present, you gain the opportunity to choose what steps you take. When we turn a blind eye to the parts of ourselves that are seeking out change, and those parts of us that wish to be expressed—we lose sight of our potential growth. In this way, when we attempt to take those steps towards our desired outcomes, we often go in the wrong direction. Being where we are is the best thing that we can do for ourselves, for how can man arrive if he never starts. At times, in a non-religious sense, we create a present hell, while chasing some future heaven. Making what is currently happening act as a mundane means to the future. Without realizing that there is no future to chase or even be a part of. All that is, happens within the present moment, and *if we wait until the future to start building what we want today, then it'll never be completed.*

The importance of presence is to be aware that the path must be walked. If we fail to take the steps necessary in the present, then our future will be filled with the obstacles we failed to see today.

NO ONE CAN JUDGE YOU MORE THAN YOU JUDGE YOURSELF

I've come to realize that no one has the ability to cast judgment on you, but you. We live in a world that is highly social, and often we define our own personhood based on how we interact with those around us. This said, when it comes to the comparison we place ourselves under, it is at most times misplaced. We need to realize how comparison truly takes away from our individuality. It's as if part of who you are needs to be in reference to who I am, in order to be valid. To provide yourself with your own sense of validity, is the only way to have it in truth. When we solely depend on the external world to govern our internal world, we are only adding to our dependence on circumstance. When it comes to being judged and judging others, we are our biggest critics. If we don't believe someone's judgment of us, we are not judged. This is not to say if you feel something when you are judged that it is the truth. The truth is within the deepest thoughts and opinions that we have about who we are. To say that other people's judgement is a representation of the judgement we have on ourselves, is to say that we often don't bring ourselves within our own connotation. Instead, we allow the world and others to define who we are, without acknowledging that we indeed know ourselves best. This isn't to say don't be honest with yourself in your times of naivety, rather understand your perspective's contribution to the life you live.

If you want to live your own life, then it should be lived via your perspective and your love. For if we are not well equipped with our own foundation, then we will often collapse or find it in the world around us, rather than the world within. When it comes to our losses, we are noted to harp on who we are, as if some external thing defines it. By contrast, when something positive occurs, it is as fleeting as we are insistent that negativity needs to be focused on more than positively. We need to understand how the color of our emotions contributes to our worldview. If we never cheer for who we are or what we do, we will always be in a performance for the world around us. I think it's far more important and worthwhile to do things for how they make you feel inside, not what they do for you outside. This is not to say abandon your job or whatever you need to survive, but know that life is much more than possession. Life is everything you are and what you experience, but most of all, the person experiencing it.

Expression

A WORLD WITHOUT WORDS

Once we recognize the role connotation has on the lives we live, then it's our responsibility to dispel our bias. We often attribute certain negative characteristics to our situations and to ourselves. We contribute to making what once just was, victim to who we currently are. Not saying we don't often have justification for the actions and feelings we exhibit. Rather, sometimes these actions do more harm than good by perpetuating our ill feeling. Once we can take a step forward from the mind long enough to realize we are not the mind. We grant ourselves an opportunity to exist beyond the words we have for everything around us. Living in a world without words isn't saying do not speak, it's saying listen to the world, rather than your connotations. Sometimes, the negativity we face is let in via our relationships to the words that we place upon them. Many things are as they are, and they should remain as such. For when we place labels on what is, the label is what it becomes. Correspondingly, when we place these labels on ourselves, then we too become restricted by the words we use to define who we are.

I find that who we are in a real sense, is beyond any word or meaning that we attempt to place upon it. This is to say that the best way to learn about who you are, is not in your attempt to define yourself. Rather, your willingness to listen to the parts of you which are abundant in your

190

actions, and in your thoughts. When we force ourselves into such simple restrictions, *the only complexity is in our inability to see our own*. Many of us have more than we could ever imagine within us, and our lack of allowance is what keeps us in the same place we were in before. I believe that thought is a powerful tool, only once you have it at your disposal. Otherwise, everything we see and encounter will be victim to our own negative perspectives.

Expression

The ongoing conversation

The blighted banter one is engaged

The serene tune from which *you* are made

How *you* agree to hold

In most times unknowing

When you don't let *you*, do the showing

What we desire remains where we are

And is illusive when you look so far

For it's not without

One loves within

But through the count

Whenever *you* begin

To love yourself and the chatter

And learn to enforce the things that matter

To *you*

NOTHING IS FOREVER

If no time is taken to take in the time, then it will be gone with our potential appreciation. When we are negligent of what needs to be appreciated within what is, we lose what could be. Each moment's good and bad can create a new foundation for us to stand on. When we are faced with troubling times, a person should not merely wait for them to pass in a subtle way. Instead, pass it within ourselves, to bring ourselves to the level of our conflict, and allow ourselves to become present in the moment. Letting go of our expectation for things to be a certain way, is the only way to create something new. For if we only rest upon what was, then what is, will never be a part of the moment. The strength we gain from actually being in the moment, is humorously not gained in our conflict. It is gained by not attempting to exercise control of the world around you. *What we attempt to control, control us.* We attach ourselves to the idea of our own control to the point where when we aren't, we punish ourselves. There are things which are within our influence certainly. However, these things will not be realized unless we learn how to be in the moment. Noting that we will never be in the moment, if we cannot at first influence ourselves.

To say nothing is forever, is to say that we need to learn to let moments go. Appreciating them for the time they took up, *not the time they no longer occupy*. In a way,

193

learning to have no preference in what is, allowing yourself to be as you are regardless of circumstance. You will find that in times of general stress, you free yourself by remembering that you decide what you can handle. If you can imagine a version of yourself which can handle a situation, then in a way it should be considered handled. *As long as you can handle yourself.* There is no moment you experience that is void of you. So, if you *can* contribute positively to the moment, then what is the justification for our lack of presence in the matter. If a new experience is desired, then we must make ourselves new.

Section Six:

*PerSpec*Tive

What makes a viewpoint correct? If man sees in the world what he carries in his heart, what will you carry? Do you have a choice?

Much of what we experience is due to our viewpoint, and if not our view, then the one viewing it. If we can learn to change the way we look, then we will often change what we fin

Perspective

It is only once your consciousness expands further than your eye can see, that one realizes the insignificance of a singular existence. We are not great simply because we are different, rather great because we tend to be individuals in a populous world. However, in small fashion, all of us are victims and recipients to the ordeals and blessings of life. We are all led astray from the unpredictable, the aspects of our view that plague existence. Existence, however, should be taken with a grain of salt. For it is only the fool who can live negligent all the movement around him. Sometimes steps must be taken outside the self in order to see value. What I've found is that there is none. We are both nothing and infinite all in the same second; it is our focus that generates all the difference. We often focus on the small and miss too much. Takehiko Inoue once said, "Preoccupied with a single leaf you will miss the tree, preoccupied with a single tree you will miss the forest"[12].

One can only worry while hyper focused. it is those who squint their eyes in search that have obscured vision. The harder one looks for a leaf, the more the forest will be lost. Time works in the same way, the more occupied with the second, the easier the hour slips by. Relax the eye to see an unstressed world. Some things aren't good or bad, rather a decision created from the minds of the past. For the moment has no connotation, it just is what it seeks to be. In life, perspective is far more important than any material item that we can consume. To be able to shift perspectives is to be able to put on a new pair of glasses at which to see what has yet to be. The reality of it, however, is that it can be hard to alter one's perspective in a matter of seconds. Perspective is engraved into our minds from the moment we enter this world. That is to say, in all matters of view we must be present to prepare for the change. Without patience, we abandon what could be, so the point is to give yourself the time to grow into what you wish.

Time

Since the dawn of our existence, man has kept track of chronology, what we know currently as time. This began with simple night and day and progressing into specific increments we base our growth off of. The industrial revolution also had a major contribution to time as we know it—however, the time we know as "Time" is nothing but an illusion. Time is a method of creating identity and keeping it set in a moment. We established something so life could be recalled, as if there really is some kind of past. When in reality, the present moment is all that can be. It's the only point where change can occur and choices can be made. We only interact with the now. However, many may argue that time has too much value placed on it. Forcing people to create false, idealistic and impulsive personalities, that prove to be the root of some major issues. First off, we think that we have a lot of time to do the things we love. Then we experience what is known as life, and live as if we are going to be here forever. time and time again, we overestimate how much time we have in a real sense. Interestingly, overestimation of the nature of self is also what stunts some of our personal growth. We allow the concept of time to ferment our personal identity, allowing what we were in this "Past" to greatly impact the future.

Profound Pondering

Our identity and time do not go well together. Greek Philosopher Marcus Aurelius once said "In a little while you will have forgotten everything; in a little while everything will have forgotten you"[13] The notion that we have more time than we do, serves as a contributor to the insecurity and lack of drive we may possess in life. The truth is, in a short amount of time little of what we are doing now will matter nor be remembered. No one man can be beyond time to their knowledge. They will know not when their existence will fade, nor will they know when their memory will be skewed.

<u>The self seen</u>

If all our time is spent in wonder

How do we expect to hear the answers

Every step would seem a blunder

To profoundly gifted dancers

This is not to say don't dance

But to say dance is not a comparison

Give yourself a chance

And there will be no embarrassment

A chance at a dream

A reality spotless

Clean

Would be the clarity of our view

The self seen

THE POWER OF PERSPECTIVE

Are things truly ever just one way or another? Is that which is subject to perspective ever truly grounded in reality? or are things varied at all times? The world we inhabit is a product of the duality of good and bad. It's the platform upon which we express our perspectives. From things such as religion and the sciences, perspective is the driving force of generational change. We victimize the self in an effort to create a duality, we think our bad is in reference to our good in life. The reason we see some experiences as suffering is, at times, for the sake of seeing contrast in how our perspective influences what we experience. We call some things ugly, so others may shine. It's because people aren't free, the very notion of freedom exists. It's the duality that generates its value. It's our reference to perspective that creates the idea of worth; this worth and the self are mistakenly treated as constructs of reference. Each person, place, or thing can only be what it is. It is the entrapments of the mind, which shape our vision and cloud our judgements. We are self-deprecating in the sense that there are many possibilities within existence. And just because these possibilities exist we feel we must always brace for negativity. In some cases, we should not connote the world in the slightest or at least allow it to be painted by anyone other than ourselves. The way at which we readily accept the connotations of other people, in some ways, can strip us of part of our identity. The greatest thing

201

about being individuals is the ability to have a unique perspective. Not to say that we must differ, rather how one views themselves is more influential than how others view them. So, it's important to understand whether or not you are pulling the strings of your own perspective.

NOTHING MEANS ANYTHING

The amount of value we posit in the perspectives and viewpoints of the past and people is unbefitting. Investing part of ourselves in many avenues that aim to generate nothing for our character. This means we put part of ourselves in a place where we, in short, do not belong. We belong with ourselves, not in others, not in perception, rather in our own perspective. I feel that knowing when to invest is a life changing skill. How we invest our care is at times selfish at first, the initial care we at times have is only in relation to how we are impacted by something. The problem is, that we only care for what impacts us, when we impact ourselves more than we can ever know.

If this is "natural" how can it possibly create negativity?

It's not natural, who we are is not just us, but all the people we influence. All of those impacted by your very existence, and how you are impacted by theirs. It's the entrapments of society that cause us to poison ourselves, *by thinking we aren't the cure.* Think of all the propaganda in the world, and how we unknowingly agree to certain patterns of thought. We focus on how we are so much because society tells us how we should be. Too much of what we care about is created for us, not by us. And for this reason, it's extremely important to ground yourself in your own perspective. Not to say don't listen to the words of others, but place value in what you have, as well as realize that your view can shift at your leisure.

VALUE

The entire system is messed up. We tend to place so much of life's meaning in things that aren't worth much at all. Real things of value are the things we get for free in some sense. A great example of this misplaced gratitude is within our appreciation for those around us, as well as our appreciation for ourselves. Friends and family can come to us without cost, and our "self" is given by default. *If you have yourself, you always will have someone.* Yet, we often replace these things of value with desire, for what we do not possess. Things with high subjective value, while objectively, not having much at all. If we learn to place value in the things we do not yet have, then what we currently possess will never get the appreciation it deserves. If we constantly crave without regard for what we possess, we will never experience the moment. True gratitude is value within the self, that which surrounds it, and occupies it. Gratitude is about acknowledging the good, the things that allow us to continue being ourselves. While we are all different, I think valuing who you are is one of the most important things to experience. It has to be, because even when we dislike who we are, we still are subject to the experience of ourselves. Who we are, is what we are, so why not place our value in something that will always be with us. Material and other things aren't a representation of who we are, rather how we are seen. We are pushed to be entrapped within the physical so much that we neglect the parts of ourselves that we cannot see. To be ourselves, we have to appreciate what is within, otherwise we will be trapped in all that is outside of us. Awareness of awareness is what allows the presence of self, and there is always value in that. Love for our process of change creates a separation between the identity we create, and the identity that was created for us. We are not as we are, we are as we wish. *If we stay stuck in a state of lack, the only thing we gain is a worthless perspective.*

<u>View what you trust</u>

If it could happen, why wouldn't it?

Too caught in the bad to see the could in it

You can't trust what you view

If you don't view what you trust

The past you been through

So in the moment you must

View the world whole

Not just the part you're in

For if you let go

Then upon you, you can depend

Analysis caused by insecurity

Is the surplus of labels placed upon the world caused by insecurity? To what extent is what we do, a reflection of what we think we lack? I have begun to think we as people constantly attempt to define all that is around us, and nothing within us. *Contentment in self is what allows us to have curiosity without question.* To not take personal what is not inherent to our character. That is to say, it is often the question of one's place in the world that makes one derive their own meaning from it. *We look out to gather parts of ourselves, without realizing we are already complete.* The self isn't something we build or create, *it's something that we become aware of.* Not to say we can't change or alter who we are, but to say when we do, we just become aware of that new part of ourselves. Who we are is not defined by how the world is, but how we are, and how we react to what is presented to us. Saying that analysis is caused by insecurity in general would be a stretch. However, in regards to the self, I find that *we question most, when we feel we don't have the answer*. Oftentimes the answer is you. The answer is your commitment to yourself and understanding. We eventually realize that our questioning of our state and security implies a lack thereof. Having curiosity applies to figuring out more about who you are, questioning applies to what you currently have. What we currently have is enough; your worth isn't something you see or create. It's something you realize without reference to that which is not you.

Everything is New

    The way we allow the past to paint our lives often creates false expectations that take us away from ourselves. If we only reference the past when we are building the future, we will only recreate it. *What is not resolved will undoubtedly repeat itself, until we come to the conclusion that we are the thing that needs to be resolved.* A life filled with reference will always take you from the subject, which is your perspective. In saying this, I do not mean only care for yourself; rather, care for yourself so intently, you are forced to care for others. Just as the love we feel for others is felt by us, so will our care, and inversely our negativity. Many times, it's our mind that seeks to control the world around us, making grand predictions for the future. I myself at times have been in my head, trying to predict how an event will go or how an interaction will unfold. However, recently I've found that it does nothing but promote early suffering. The only guaranteed way to make sure you do the "right" thing in any event, is to be present enough to make the choice, when it occurs. *Our situations often aim to paint our character, not because they are inherent to us, but because we think we are inherent to them. The choice to be present gives you an opportunity to see that you are not what you encounter, you are the thing encountering them.* In this way, we must be mindful of how much we allow within our definition. Noting that it is your definition, the importance should be to make sure you're the one who makes it.

It's one thing to say that we should treat each new day like a new life, but entirely different to say that everything is new. That is, when we do get more opportunities to experience the world, we should do so in a way that invites new perspectives. I feel as if a lot of the world's beauty is lost, in our degradation of that which is familiar. The more we see something, the less we are initially curious about it. Which is why I think it's important to realize that each and every thing you encounter, only contains the depth you allow it to have in your mind. The same thing applies to ourselves when talking about what we can achieve. I find that many of the limits we think we have are self imposed, "To know it's humanly possible means you too can do it"[13]. Treating everything as if it were new is giving your life an opportunity to be yours, instead of being a repetition of the past.

Present enough to see

The way we see the world is filled with how we feel about ourselves. We often place connotations onto ourselves and what we encounter, without acknowledgement of how that impacts our experience. In this way, we deny ourselves the luxury of whatever beauty is present within the world. *While looking for anything, we often lose whatever is surrounding it, and oftentimes the thing we lose is ourselves.* When referencing how we place value onto ourselves, we often do so in reference to what is outside of us. We tell ourselves that love is outward, we forget that it's something we can possess for ourselves. *Not to say don't express it outwardly, instead we need to realize a lot of what we look for is only lost, because we don't look within ourselves.* We have to be present enough to see what is in front of us. Especially if we want to have any influence. We can't heal what we don't acknowledge, you can't capitalize on an opportunity that you can't see. *That's why the subtle importance in life should not be to find your worth, but to be present enough to see it.* We often ask ourselves questions that can only be answered and expressed in our actions. "Do I love myself?" Or things like, "What am I doing with my life?" When the answer is often laid out right behind our action. We have more value than meets the eye, especially once we realize the thing we should value most, is the thing behind them.

EVERYTHING IS NOW

Don't be patient, be present. We often get what we are looking for as soon as we become content without it. In saying this, I mean that our value is not within that which we possess, rather *the possession of ourselves*. Our value has always been in our perspective, both in thought and in application. How you see yourself tends to influence how you see the world. And if we stay within our minds, we will never see the connection. Patience with the world is a necessity, as it contributes to the patience we give to ourselves. Not to say we should wait on life to happen, rather to say that life is already happening. Our constant search for positive aspects of life often takes them away. If we only reference our lives to positive external occurrences, then we will always be governed by the world. To say that everything is now, is to say that we can only receive anything in the present. When we don't take the time to be present, then we can't see anything. Our relative understanding of the world can only be gathered, if we take the time to see it. The way we allow ourselves to live in the mind of others, when our own accommodates us so much more passively. How we reference others' opinions in our thoughts of ourselves, is unbefitting. How we express ourselves, is only as deep as we allow, and how talented we are in doing so. In acknowledging the complexity of the world, we only have greater reason to explore the complexity of ourselves. If we don't take the time to affirm the one walking our path, then there's no point in walking at all.

If we can take in the moment we have been awarded, everything outside of us will be representative of that peace. *Not because the space we occupy is peaceful, rather we are peaceful within the space we occupy.* We often project our mental restrictions onto the situations that we encounter. If we are waiting on our freedom or waiting on ourselves, then both are likely never going to arrive. Everything we will ever be is within the present moment, and if we are always waiting on life to happen, it will pass us by.

Perception of the double-edged sword

A sword with millions of edges can only be sheathed if the user becomes aware that it's still one sword

GIVE YOURSELF AUDIENCE AND YOU'LL NO LONGER NEED TO PERFORM

Our very need to be seen by others forces us to act in accordance with our perceptions, of their perceptions. That is to say that our performance in this world is often done for the sake of appearance, rather than being. Attempting to exemplify ourselves, when being ourselves is something that we can embody without effort. When we don't listen to our own internal workings, I feel like they are lost. Everything becomes a result of external factors, persons, and circumstances, when things are really as they are. Our own perspective is constantly shifting our view of the world around us. If we can recognize that our perspective dictates how we perceive things, then our effort should be placed in understanding our perspective. I find that it is quite difficult to heal what we fail to acknowledge. If we cannot acknowledge ourselves, then we can never emerge as healed people. To give oneself an audience isn't about watching the role that you play, but realizing that you are not a role to be played. You are a person filled by your own individuality and complexity. For this reason, we must give ourselves an open ear and a watchful eye, for we don't learn in effort but in willingness to listen. Once we listen to ourselves, we will learn validation and love are things that can be given to yourself. Once we start to watch over ourselves, we will see that what we need isn't to be experienced by others, but to experience our own lives. If

214

all we do is live in reference, then how will we ever be the subject? I think that self-love truly starts once you open yourself to the idea of your perfect imperfection. If we are the ones who can see all of our internal workings and feelings, then we must also be the ones to validate them.

WE ARE WHAT WE EXPERIENCE

The longer we allow ourselves to identify with our minds, the more we will be subject to its bias. Not to say that the mind is bad, rather to understand that the mind is a tool not a counsel. Our deep-rooted association with our thoughts allows us to be governed by them, and the thoughts of others. In saying this I hope to stress the idea that we have the power to influence what we think. In saying we are what we experience, I mean to say that we often project our feelings into the world around us. If we aren't conscious of this however, then we are lost in the very effort to find ourselves. Everything in a way becomes a reflection of our internal works. We find ourselves uncomfortable at times, not because we are uncomfortable within the world, but we are uncomfortable within ourselves. As long as we are governed by our own bias, the world we experience will be more of what we are, than what it is. If you cannot accept yourself, then you cannot accept the world, because you are in fact a part of the world. This is why I feel as if affirmation is one of the most important things when it comes to yourself. If we cannot walk the path, then there is no point in thinking about the outcome. If we cannot affirm the one walking it, then there is no point in walking it at all. When we get too preoccupied with what we do, we often lose track of the one that's doing it, and the one that we are doing it for. In placing your focus and awareness back onto yourself, you open the door back to your own understanding. After some time, through contrast and acceptance, we obtain understanding of others.

Allowing yourself to be is also something that is extremely important. Not to say that you think there is no part of you that needs to change. Rather, love yourself while changing. In this way, our value is no longer based on the world around us and starts being about us within the world. Not particularly in a selfish way, but in a way of understanding that we are what we experience.

THE ONLY WAY TO OVERCOME IS TO ACCEPT

How can you reach a goal you don't think is there? How can you confront a problem without recognizing there is one to confront? If we never take a moment to look upon what we experience, then we will only live in reference to memory. The more we allow our thoughts to occupy our reality, the more we will be dictated by thought alone. The issue with this thought is not its application, but its potential influence. When we do not pay heed to what we feed ourselves, we will often grow in ways that we don't find befitting. To say the only way to overcome is to accept, is to say that unless we lower our guard enough to be who we are, we will feel attacked by the world around us. If we never stop playing defense, then we will always feel like we are being attacked. If we always feel like we are being attacked, we will begin to attack those around us. Not in a literal sense of the word, rather in a sense of projection. Bringing our internal problems into the external world, then perpetuating them through our perspective. Compounding upon a negative experience to create a negative world for ourselves. I feel as though accepting anything is to accept yourself outside of it or within it. Either way I feel it is integral for us to be content with who we are, so we can genuinely influence our actions and our outcomes. Change can only occur when we accept things as they are. More so, change becomes natural when we accept our role in our own change. To get anywhere we must start where we are, not where we are going. *Reluctance to accept yourself, is reluctance to experience yourself.*

The cycles of life remain as they are as long as we remain as we are. Our perspective guides our thoughts, actions and life, and if we don't recognize our own cycles we will always be a part of larger ones. Our revolutions must start in our own minds, at our own time, and where we are. If this does not occur, then it will never occur, and the change we desire will always be more of a thought, than it is a reality.

All we stand to gain

We've lost as soon as we think victory is near

For it isn't close, it's right here

When we expect to win

We lose our ability to decide

For its not chance

But in presence where victory resides

If we could put ourselves beyond defeat

Then victory wouldn't be a thought

It would be where we are

Simple and plain,

If we live in lack

We lose all we stand to gain

DON'T LEAVE SPACE FOR DOUBT

If we don't occupy our mind, it will be occupied by things that are not us. In saying this, I extend that our foundations are either built by circumstance or by intention. When we are intent with our growth and our aspirations, we are able to be more consistent in our pursuit of that which we want. We must in this same way feed ourselves, in a mental sense, things that will allow us to grow in a good way. Our growth has always been characteristic of our ability to give ourselves what we need, and reject what we don't. When we vest ourselves in negativity, we cannot possibly think a positive version of ourselves will emerge. Doubt in this way, is having faith in a negative outcome or identification with issues, rather than solutions. To say don't leave space for doubt, is to say that we need to learn to take up our own space. *Sometimes we get so caught up within the idea of who we are that we fail to add more.* Giving ourselves space, at least in mind, permits us to transcend what we have previously taught ourselves. A great deal of us have been conditioned to think negatively about who we are and what we do. If we aren't at the forefront of our own desires, we tend to fall into a process of self neglect. Not to say that our entire mind should be fixed on our own progression, but it should at the least have us within it.

The separation we create between who we are now, and who we will be in the future often creates our separation from our desires. We think that we are in a sense finite, not fit for what we wish to achieve to the extent of inaction. When we are unable to act, our goals become mere thoughts. We must in a real way, give ourselves a better opportunity to genuinely move towards our desires. I feel as though we have to have a large amount of faith in ourselves in order to do anything real. I think a certain amount of authenticity will allow you to be in the world, without forcing yourself to be a certain way. The love we have for ourselves should be rooted in love, not in condition. We often place conditions on ourselves to do practically everything. "I need to be more confident before I… I need to work on myself before I can…" without recognizing that the work you need to do is always in the moment, not in the mind.

LIFE'S SYMPHONY

It is so beautiful at times how each part makes the whole significant. It is vast beyond recognition. Yet, it is finite at the same time. In some ways we people are like a lens which shifts focus each second. To have control in any sense, is to control your view, to be able to shift it to the level of whatever it is you desire. We have a troubling habit of making our dreams larger than we are, and by doing so they become larger than we are. We have to understand that our life is curated by our perspective, not entirely our environment. The vastness of the world holds nothing to the vastness of the individual perspective. We all live different lives while looking upon the same exact things. So we must realize that what we experience is subject to our perspective, and what we allow ourselves to consume. It's as though at any time we can pull from our depths the antidote to any ailment, or issue. All sickness begins at first in the mind, not in a sense of genuine ailments, *but in a sense of man-made ills*. Too often we allow our true self to play the role of a backseat driver. We often hide from the very parts of us that could cure our illness. It would seem however, that we still allow this "self" to be captain of our ship, so long as we don't bring him forward to anyone's sight. *Maybe one day we will realize that safe driving is worth the risk of being seen, especially if it is by ourselves,* and especially if our path has to be walked by us. As we bring darkness to light it too will show its vibrance.

PerSpecTive

Sometimes things are only dark due to the shadow we cast over them.

Section Seven:

Wholeness

*The most freeing realization is that **everything is
everything**. If we are only part, we will never be whole. And
if we only look at part of ourselves, we will never
understand the totality of our being.*

YOU HAVE TO LET YOURSELF GO

If we keep the same thoughts, we will keep the same perspective. If we keep the same perspective, we will keep the same thoughts and actions. It is important to realize how much our thoughts condition our world and our experience. The way we think impacts how we feel, which shapes what we see, which influences how we feel. If we don't create some type of break in this cycle, who we are will always be defined by who we were. Letting yourself go is about renewal. It is about giving yourself enough love in the moment to actually be in the moment. When we don't embrace where we are, it is often because we wish to be somewhere else. If we cannot accept what is, then we can never have something that is new. *To let go of anything, we must in some way be conscious enough to see what it is we wish to let go of.*

When it comes to the self, I think we don't realize how much our view of who we are is compounded by our actions. When we act in accordance with our own perceived inadequacies, they become more inherent to who we are as people. The point isn't to live in our negativity, but to be present enough to walk away from it. To let yourself go is to know that who you are is only here and now. The past is indeed the past and who you are is subject to as much change as you allow. The idea of holding firmly onto who you are is, I feel, what contributes to stagnation.

Profound Pondering

If we hold onto the self, it almost implies that if we let go there would be nothing left.

However, this is not the case, letting yourself go is an act of faith. It's the realization that who you are is always here, regardless of whether or not you hold on. If you recognize yourself holding onto parts of yourself that do not contribute to who you are, then holding on is counterintuitive. If we allow parts of ourselves that seek our change to make up the whole of our character, then holding on is what is causing us suffering. I find that the only way to overcome the negative stagnation of the self, is to realize that you can be any way you think yourself to be. Sometimes telling yourself you can't achieve something is making it so. We find too much comfort in what is "Known" to the point that we adopt a definition of ourselves and feel as if we have to change everything to change a part. This is to say that we allow our parts to define the whole too often. If we were to allow our negative parts to be just parts, then we would be far more suited to change them. Letting yourself go is, in a way, allowing yourself to be seen. Allowing each part, good and bad, to come to light so you can intentionally let go and or get rid of what is not serving you. If you keep the parts of yourself that seek change hidden or held onto, then they won't be seen or let go of, and you will never change for the better.

EXPECT NOTHING, GAIN EVERYTHING

When we allow what we desire to be separate from the value we have for ourselves, we allow it to be beyond our expectation. In being beyond this expectation, we are allowed to be present enough with the life we live, to create a life within it. I find that when we allow our lives to be lived beyond our expectation, what occurs is always more than we could ever ask for. The practice of letting go is what allows us to attract what we desire. Holding on implies that if we were to let go, it would leave us. Letting go is implying that that success we crave, is in some way part of us. *Letting go is what makes it stay.* There is so much in the world that is unknown to us, especially what has yet to occur. To impress expectation is to subtly make yourself dependent on outcome. This is not at all to say that what you put effort towards will only be given by random chance. Rather, recognizing that when we invest too much of ourselves in what has yet to occur, we lose a lot of what is present for us in this moment. The present is where everything is going to occur with regard to our goals and aspirations. I find that it is more valuable to invest your attention and energy into the moment, so you can actively build what you want to "expect". When you expect nothing, you are likely to create exactly what you desire in the sense of being there to do it. Our mind, if used improperly, can take us away from the present. Especially when we allow ourselves to be in this future anxiety about what might happen. If we want to be successful in the near future, it isn't about having expectations of that success. It's about doing what you need to be fully present, where you can actually take action. As well as be outside of your mind long enough to find comfort in who you are, without what you desire.

We shouldn't have to jump through hoops to find some appreciation for what we have. We shouldn't need to have certain expectations set in the future, in order to enjoy where we are. All of this is not to say expectation is unwarranted, rather, to say when you expect nothing, everything you receive is a true gift. When doing the things you love, it's about what it does to you inside, not what it does for you outside.

Freedom

If we all must abide by the decree of the mad, how can we call ourselves sane? We are neglectful of the state of power, in the place all but forsaken by those who began it. We are not free in most ways. To exercise free will in a real sense, is nothing but calculations placed upon the risk that is existence. Not to say that hierarchy is all that entraps us, for it is the fear and tradition that forces us to repeat the mistakes of the past. The past revelations of a time, become the common sense of the now. Even the top must have guidance to allow such selfishness to be displayed from its being. They are stricken with identity and ego, as are we. In the most negative of avenues, ego is the root of the issue. It is because we believe that we are, that we can. To believe in most senses is to give up freedom. To believe is to doubt for if we knew we would not need to believe. The distinction here breeds separation between the men on each side of the coin, both convinced by ego that they are on a dollar.

We pull worth from the outside. We are not free. We analyze our lives more than they are lived. We are not free. We have power but "not individually", we are not free. It is a waste to not attempt to be free, for some will always be better than none. If it is to be given, that it is theirs to give and not ours to take. We mirage our skies to honor those who were once our captors, we are not free. Given the power to create only to have it restricted, we are not free. If we were free, then there would be no discussion of the word. The chains on our being are inflicted nonetheless, all from a source no matter what we are not free. To live by their standards in our minds is to be good, We are not free. To even possess morals is to be restricted in a good way. To have freedom is to imply the captivity of others.

I think that freedom is all that is, not in a sense of our restrictions. Rather, the freedom awarded to the individual who unburdens himself. Freedom is not about what contains us but what we contain within ourselves. So, to achieve freedom we must free ourselves from our own critical perspective. Then, begin to realize that what we see in the world is what we carry in our hearts. So when you carry your fear, you see the causes. However, when you carry your heart, you are granted a life of freedom.

Harmonized Discord

To begin, I should add context to what it means to exist within harmonious discord. A jazz concert. At first when encountering things typically thought mundane or boring, we fail to see the value in experiences. We allow faulty expectations to shackle us from doing as we please. As the musicians begin to play it seems as if we fail to see something so vividly clear. Each player acts as their own band, contributing in full what it means to be an individual. The full individual gives to the mass. It's as if by following your own path, you inspire others to do the same. While the standard view of this would cause people to think of chaos, it is in fact the opposite. A collection of separate parts making a better whole, Jazz is the player and the players all at once. What jazz is, is the life that breeds harmony through seemingly random acts of chaos. The grace of it teaches that all that is, does not need strict order to have just and good reasoning. Regardless of connotation, jazz is the compilation of separate passions. However, it does not act as the will of one man, when put together. The individual is not lost in the slightest; he is only completed. The more we support life as we know it, the more likely life is to support us. This answer we allow to be unknown, it is but the mind of man that traps him in the falseness of his reality. Expression is freedom. The path of man breeds suffering, and to suffer is to be human. To be a human is to be part of this harmony within discord, the difference, being but the projection of the mind.

FLOWING WITH LIFE

To what extent should we let things go? Should we take responsibility for the feelings we have? We all suffer from attacks of the mind, mainly constructed by ungrounded nonsense—which springs us into unrealistic analysis of the external world. That is to say, we overthink, or more so overthink about the thoughts that lead to overthought. *When determining what truth is within our anxieties,* we often find it lies in the lack of responsibility we take for ourselves and our conscious. As well as the over zealous amount of responsibility placed on the subconscious. It's the dichotomy that we've generated between those two that hold both back, making them unable to be what they could be. It is my current understanding that the subconscious is just a collection of what we've been conscious of. These are imprints on that self that we have accepted to be truly us. Instead of allowing these parts of us to change, we selfishly view them as essential. When in truth they are a projection of mental issues onto oneself.

We need to be more aware of what we allow ourselves to consume in the spectrum of positive and negative. The mind is a sponge, and we must care for it, otherwise negativity will cloud our judgments of ourselves, and the world around us. The world is a terrible place if you only allow yourself to see that aspect of it. Not to say what occurs in this world is good, rather it contains too much negativity for one person to bear. It can easily overwhelm those who tend to be more empathetic towards things that exist outside of themselves. What we need to do, is tend to the self and go with the path that gives us the most self respect and peace. That which is not in your hands, should escape your mind. We must do what we can with what we have. Address your issues and traumas directly, which does not mean to allow it to attach itself to who you are in the moment or ever. We are far more vast than we know and contain more potential than we'll ever show. Be there for you.

Be the Life

We look for life too much for us to be able to live it; we neglect the fact that life is the whole process, not just the good aspects that we search for. As a matter of fact, the good parts are far more vast than we are able to consciously think about. *To be life is much more than seeing it*, while being lost in analysis, we fail to truly see. We attempt to listen, without being able to hear. Peace lies within the uncounted second, the world where we don't force ourselves to play a part, but allow ourselves to play it. Life is thought more than it is lived, and our mind plagues what we think to be the self. The mind has a lot less control than we give it, if you were to simply prompt your mind to move, it would not. If you were to ask it to think of your next thought, it would never be produced. The problem is we are the observer, acting as if we are the thought itself. Life is a constant happening, not an instance or an event. Who we are and the lives we live are not a contradiction, rather a representation of what is, and what could be. We are stuck between the past and possibility, it's up to us to be able to see that. *There is so much to life that remains unwritten and the main thing we fail to write is ourselves.*

Each day should be viewed as a new life, as we often get lost in the large scale of time. We can only "have time" in the present, so our preoccupation with the past and future, at times, gets rid of our present potential. The world in our heads is not for us to conquer, rather for us to build upon. We must in some ways plant ourselves and take care of whatever sprouts. You don't plant a bad seed, you plant in bad soil, or you take poor care of what presents itself. All that we have is here and now, whatever neglect you've given yourself can't be taken away at all. However, new care can be added, you cannot alter that past but, you can create the future. If we only live life in reference, will we ever truly be the subject? *We must be the life we live, life comes from us not at us.*

Wholeness

THE POWER OF THE PRESENT

The mind often takes us away from ourselves, more than it allows us to be. In our mind, we cannot be in the present moment, and in many ways that is all that is. When we reference time, we are really referencing a past or future present. All that ever happens, happens in the present, and that is where we are able to make the most change to ourselves and the world around us. When trapped in our mind in regards to ourselves, we often displace our growth. The more we attempt to find ourselves in reference to the past, the more we repeat the behaviors of the past. With finding ourselves in the future, *we disregard the power of our present self to be exactly as we imagine*. It is the fact that we treat the self like something we have to chase—like something that will be good in the future. *We have to understand that our relationship to ourselves cannot have its foundation in a time that has yet to happen, or a time passed. It must happen now.* You can never get to your goal if you don't start from where you are, with what you have. It's not about how much you have in reference to others either, rather how much you have in reference to yourself. Living in reference can do nothing for us but take us away from ourselves, and the present moment.

If you want your desires to be in reality, why do you keep them in your mind? Action is a present thing, and the only opportunity we have to instantiate ourselves into the

238

world. All great ideas and inventions were all first thought, then acted upon, and we must do the same. For example, If we feel like we need to be more kind, we don't just hope in the future we will be kinder. We act now so that in this future we dream of, kindness will be there. I believe your success is mainly constrained by your ability to invest reality into yourself and your ideas. If you don't think you can do something, chances are you won't try or you won't invest yourself into what it is you desire. When you put nothing into the present moment, you get nothing out. When you put yourself into what it is you want, you find more of yourself. So why waste time living in your head when you can live in the world?

Wholeness

To wake up

It's not something we do

Rather a choice we make

You think it's untrue

Until ignorance breaks

A million pieces of a shattered ego

Yet what you are still remains

For you are not just what you think

But he who holds the frame

And we must love it all the same

To wake is not to start thought

But to bring awareness

Caught in yesterday's dilemma

not present for what today is

To see the world and smile

Is to share one with the self

And if we only shared more

There would be lesser concerns for health

THE EFFORTLESS INBETWEEN

Our effort to find is, at times, the very reason that we lose. It's as if by searching for more, we lose all that we already possess. When the thing we are looking for is ourselves, we are the thing that's lost. Our presence in the world is not characterized by our thoughts, rather our awareness. *How much we can see is void of what we are looking for.* In the search for meaning, we often lose our own. How can you find yourself anywhere but where you are? This is not to say we don't learn about ourselves over time; rather, *you don't learn in effort to find, but in willingness to listen.* In the present moment, your perspective is your strength. In a way it seems like the world attempts to pacify that which is already at peace. Our relative comfort with the world is not characterized by the world, it's who we are and our relation to it. The cure to our ailments is, at times, found in the realization that we can be that which heals the self. Between the past and future lie all the spoils of now—and these spoils are, at times, the stepping stones to our passions. The progressive realization of a worthy ideal isn't about waiting either, it's about bringing your ideal future to where you are now. This is why I believe efforts to tend to the future often cause displacement with what you can do now to build that future. If we don't learn to love who we are now and where we are now, then it won't be present. Life is filled with what you give it, and if you yourself are full of that which you want to be present in your life, then as long as you're here it too will be present.

BE WHERE YOU ARE

If we could simply be in the center of now, then we would be able to see where we are going. If we aren't present enough to see our steps, we are more likely to go in the wrong direction. Some of the obstacles that we face in life are not just due to the world and chance, rather ourselves in our lack of presence. Our situations become our defining principles, when we believe we are our situations. If we are unable to be where our feet are, we will look everywhere else to find out who we are. To say be where you are, is to say that the only place where you can be is here. If we stay in our minds, when will we truly be within the world? If we don't take the time to be present, then when will we meet others? When will we experience *it*? To be within the mind in this way, is akin to being in another world, for if we always live in the connotation of the mind, we will never see things for what they are. This is not to say that thinking has no place, or to say that the mind is useless. The mind's application is not in defining who we are but understanding the world around us. If we cannot separate the mind from our definition, we will never see the world, so much as we see ourselves. The presence that we give to ourselves allows us to see the world, void of our bias. Presence also gives us the opportunity to change the way we think, to better accommodate who we are into where we are.

Wholeness

When we are present we have a choice, a choice to see that which we keep our mind tended to. When we take this step forward, we can begin at once to replace our old thoughts with new. Once again, allowing ourselves, and the world we see, to become as new as our thoughts. For if nothing changes if nothing changes, *you won't see the good of the world in focusing on the bad within yourself.* The only place where you can begin to change the negative aspects of yourself is always where they are most prominent, the present moment. If we vest more positivity in who we are, and in being ourselves, then we will see more in the world around us. A negative mind creates a negative world, and a positive mind creates a positive one. This again is not to say that negative things won't happen, rather you will not become negative along with the things that come into your view. It's important at the minimum to be present enough to realize that you aren't anywhere but where you are. To be here is to allow other things to be there, *to accept yourself is to accept the world.*

Profound Pondering

THE JOURNEY IS NEVER ENDING

To live is to embrace the idea that we do not know what is yet to come. If we were able to predict the future, what interest would we have in the present? This said, many of us tend to try to be future predictors. As if we know what will happen at every twist and turn. We do this to the point where we vest our value in our mental projection of the future. Many find that it is important to have desire, but it is also important to realize your desires are not all you are. When we all walk our paths, it's not about what comes into your possession, but how much of yourself you realize is in your own. When we walk through life thinking that our path has ceased or that the path is not ongoing, we get complacent. There always exists an opportunity for change and for renewal. If we can grant ourselves this small liberty, then we would be as free as we are willing to continue to move forward. Time waits for no one, and *it's at times a selfish act to not act for yourself*. We assume that we still have time, or that tomorrow will provide us with the same opportunities that we have today. Doing your best isn't about doing what you think you should do today, but doing what you can with what you have, today. The work and passion that we give to every moment, is the joy and relief we feel when we finally reap what we sow. Therefore, to continue to move forward and embrace the newness of each day, is akin to continuing to sow yourself into life. In time, what we vest in our

245

Wholeness

experience today will serve as a greater foundation for who we have yet to become.

There is no point in making our happiness dependent on some stagnant idea. Even if who we are is changing, we can still love it as if we were at our final goal. You can't hate yourself into something better, and nothing changes if nothing changes. Some might say that they like where they are or they like their circumstances. However, the path is not just about where you are, it's about who you are and who you can become.

Profound Pondering

<u>The height of the stars</u>

The height of the stars does not shift

And we aren't much higher from where we sit

The race is won by slowing it

Not to a stop, But to a permanent end

For a race need not drop

When victory is a word not a friend

A mental relation of value

When that is possible for all

It's to love yourself for your differences

And stay on pace

Or listen to the crowd

And leave without a trace

Not one of people

But thoughts and ideas

And we'll see it next time we see you

Not from how you look

But from how you see

for if you think you're above

Down is what you'll be

Wholeness

YOU DON'T NEED EVERYTHING, TO BE SOMETHING

The way we wait to feel good about who we are often contributes to nothing but a repetitive sense of lack. Our focus on material, labels, or external ideas to find a sense of strength within, is the source of our weakness. We are not great by what we possess, but by what we are. The more we distance our value and pride in who we are from ourselves, the more we will find dependence on outcomes to be at peace. If peace is not found but created, then all we are doing is failing to create our own peace. Failing to create a space for who we are, to genuinely and authentically exist within the world. We ask questions like, "What place do I have in this world?" *Without recognizing we are already taking up space.* The objective is to be present enough to take up the space that you occupy actively. The guard we place in our mind about issues and obstacles, are the obstacles themselves. The fight we face outside is only as troublesome as we are internally troubled.

It is important to find out who you are via your own definition, and act in alignment with that idea. You might not find yourself distinct, but *rest assured that your truth and beauty, lie beyond the ugliness of your thoughts about your condition.* We must begin to implant and counteract all the negativity that we have fed ourselves through our

248

lifetime and create something new. We are taught to depend on circumstance to be happy, to be at peace, to have love for who we are. When all of those things are characteristic of being a person, of being human.

There are circumstances and problems that we will face, but even after we overcome them, the issue rests within how we face ourselves. You don't need everything to be something. This is a simpler way of saying: *you are already somebody.* We often displace our own value in what we can imagine ourselves to be or some possibility, without recognizing that it is all possible. How we limit ourselves is often represented in our reluctance to venture into the unknown aspects of life. We think we know how we ought to be, without knowing that we must be the ones acting in order to achieve that possibility.

BEAUTY DOESN'T ESCAPE THE MOMENT, WE DO

If we know our perspective influences what we perceive, then we must note that the absence of beauty is often the absence of self. Not to say that you are the source of beauty; rather, when we are too occupied with our internal troubles, we fail to see external and internal beauty. In many ways, beauty can never escape the moment, only we can. When we look outside or at some grand work of art, it never changes, at least in a grand way. However, time and time again we treat it as if it were nothing, while at other times we treat it with the acknowledgement it deserves. What I have realized is, the lack of acknowledgement of the beauty of life is often caused by a lack of acknowledgement of our own beauty. We constantly live in reference to this idea that we must be many ways, before we are the way we desire. That we must undergo many trials and tribulations before we are able to give ourselves the clarity and love we genuinely crave from every part of our existence. When you let yourself be in the moment, void of preoccupation with the self, the only thing that can truly be present is beauty. Even some of the ugliest things are beautiful by how they make everything around them shine brighter and brighter. This is not to say live in contrast, but to say that there exists beauty in all mundane things we pass over. There exists negativity and bad within what can be viewed of course, this is not at all to be negligent of the ill roots of many of our persons. Rather, to acknowledge the beauty that is our own self, the beauty that is just in being a person and having the ability to see/be beautiful.

When I say beauty, I do not solely mean some connotation of people or place. Rather, a recognition of the relationship one must have with the world around them in order to see the world around them. When we are too caught by the things we run from, we are unable to see all that we pass by for what it is. These fleeting images that we often overlook contain the answer and peace that many of us crave. At times, rushing only makes things appear as if they were going faster, when the reality is they are not. *We must create peace where we are, otherwise we will only find it where problems are not.* If we are anything alike, then our problems are not so much the world around us. They are borne of our own prescription and poisons we drink daily, believing they are remedies for our mental undoing. The overzealous focus on the negative, often overrides the positive. Not to say that we shouldn't acknowledge the shadow, but to say we must begin to be the body.

LAUGH AT YOUR OWN HUMOR

If we always wait till the audience applauds, before we applaud ourselves, then we risk performing forever. I think part of the reason we at times find ourselves stuck, is because we convinced ourselves we must be a way, in order to be ourselves. That we must subscribe to a way of acting, in order to love and accept ourselves as we are. This is not to neglect some code of ethics, or to be negligent of how you impact others. At the very least it's to be acutely aware of how you impact yourself in your lack of appreciation. In a lot of ways, we must learn to laugh at our own humor. Not just in a sense of comedy and general humor, but in a sense of appreciating our own authenticity. Our individuality is a key component of our own genuine success, if we are to succeed, we must be the ones to do it. Any gain we have while being authentic to ourselves seems like less of a gain, and more of a regaining of part of self. Achievements are not merely external but internal, it's not about what you do, but what it does for you. The longer we take to realize this the longer we will only be playing part in the grand scheme that is life. We limit ourselves to the limitations of others, and define our love for ourselves, by how others love us. When we are deprived of love in an external sense, we must begin to lean on the love we have within. If that love is not present, then we must begin at once to love who we are void of what we do. For how we interact with the world is representative of how we interact

252

with the self. This is not to say, do anything and love yourself, but to say *love yourself enough to choose actions which make that love easy.*

Laughing at your own humor in a real sense, is to live in a world that accommodates your own happiness. I find that we at times exist in our feelings and thoughts too much to embrace the possibility of new ones. We convince ourselves of the role we play so adamantly that we forget it is something we play. Not to say who we are is not genuine, but rather who we are is not static. We are not static people, we are people who exist in change, from each experience, each interaction, each day, we are new. So, the perspective and appreciation we have for our new selves, is something I feel must be renewed and reevaluated each moment. Not in stress or in effort, in listening to the ways in which we are undone, by what we experience both internally and externally.

THE BEST WAY TO BREAK THE CYCLE IS TO NOT BE WITHIN IT

If what isn't resolved always repeats, then our resolution will only be found, when we don't repeat the past. Many of the cycles that we endure are more internal than they are external, and if we cannot recognize this, we will always be chasing our own tail. What we run from has already caught us, in this case the thing we run from is our former self. Allowing each day to be filled with a subtle disdain for who we were, rather than love for who we have yet to become and who we are now. If we can't build from a standpoint of love for who we are, then our life will be filled with the same experiences that caused our undoing. To be within the cycle is not to say that if we live a cyclic lifestyle we are in the wrong. If our objective is not to change what is occurring both outside and within then breaking our cycle is not a necessary thing. However, if we find ourselves needing change or craving some type of resolution, we are better off finding it within than without. To say, the best way to break the cycle is to not be within it, is to say that we must become new. This is not to say forget who we are, or disregard everything that has happened in the past. Rather, be so invested in the moment, that your future will be based more on present choice, than random "chance". Every day is a chance, an opportunity for us to be present, and make the choices that lead us to ourselves.

Profound Pondering

To make decisions that allow us to find ourselves where we are, rather than where we are going. Why should we have to wait to be the best version of ourselves? *Why do we treat our change as if it is necessary yet approach it like we have no part to play.*

If we do not take an active role in the choices we make, day in and day out, then we will continue to fall into the repetitive nature of our subconscious. *The only way to make new choices is to make new choices.* The only way to be able to make those choices, is to be present enough to see when you can. The subconscious will keep us on autopilot, compelling us to keep playing the role we have convinced ourselves to play. This is not to say that the role we play is a bad one, but to say that if we want change, we must be the ones to change.

YOU ATTRACT WHAT YOU ARE

What we experience in the world is often a result of what we experience in our minds. We always feel the result of our most repetitive and dominant thoughts. If we always think about what we fear, then it's not only manifested in what we experience, but how we experience ourselves. The world often reflects what we project, and what we project is always in reference to what we have within. At a time, we must take into consideration what strings are pulling our actions.

We often are unaware of what is pulling our strings until they are pulled. So, the responsibility isn't to be obsessed in search, but to address what we know and be open to learn more. We have to be present with ourselves to see what takes us away from the moment. If we fear success, we will find things to fear within our success. If we have faith in our success, we will find the spoils of faith represented within our success. This is to say that regardless of what outcome you encounter, it is still your encounter. The situation always requires that you take part in recognizing how you are separate from it. This of course is not something that is blatantly available, but by definition, is present. The strings that pull us are not invisible; we are just neglecting what impacts us, through how we impact ourselves. This is why I feel it is important to ground yourself in a sense of your own love and prosperity. If we really do attract what we are, then we must first create newness within, to experience something new without.

Everything is a beginning, and everything we create starts from what's created in our minds. Of course, there are scenarios which are not in direct reference to our perspective and life choices. However, those that do fall under the jurisdiction of our perspective must have some kind of enforcer. If we are subject to what we attract, then we must take responsibility for the thing attracting. That is to say be both mindful of what you feed others as well as what you feed yourself. Many times we fail to give ourselves an accurate amount of space, to account for our own negligence. Not to say we are all unaware, but to say that the only place you find yourself, is where you are, and there is always more to find. You cannot tend to a plant, without seeing the plant for what it is, and sometimes you don't know an issue exists, until an issue presents itself. In the same light we often don't get a chance to see our growth, until we give ourselves an opportunity to. Our faith is waiting on the other side of our fear, and our love on the other side of hate. If we don't make the choice to align ourselves with that which we want, then all we will attract will be reflective of what we want to leave behind.

Wholeness

YOU ARE THE EXPERIENCE

If we ever come to a stop long enough to be outside our thoughts, we will realize that we are the only thing moving. Not in a real sense of motion, rather in a sense of perspective and self understanding. We think that the world is coming at us, when it is really coming from us. Not in a sense of our creation, in a sense of our contribution, our projection. We can live our entire lives in reference to other people or their ideas. We can do everything by the book and still find ourselves longing for something else to experience, something else to find. This search will always continue, as long as we don't realize that we are the thing that is missing. When you first get into an altercation, when someone says something to you that you dislike, you are always experienced before that something. When we come in contact with the world, we first come in contact with the conditioning we have allowed ourselves to undergo. If I myself am a negative person, and my thoughts are characteristic of negativity. When someone comes to me and says something I can interpret as negative, what will my natural reaction be? I think it is important to give ourselves enough space to actually occupy ourselves. We often limit who we are, at least in an average sense, to the extent of our own negligence. Our experience is not solely what we see in the world, but what we see within ourselves. To say let go is an invitation to the real experience of yourself. When you stop squinting your eyes, you begin to see the full picture in a greater beauty. When you stop stressing yourself about being yourself, you emerge.

To say "you are the experience" is to say that your whole life is characteristic of the perspective that you grant yourself. To grant yourself a perspective is to open the door to more than yourself, but the world around you. When we are too preoccupied with ourselves, we are in some ways unable to see the world for what it is, we see it for who we are. If we are negative, that's what we will experience most, when we are positive, parts of what we see follow suit.

FAREWELL ADDRESS

Where a path splits it two it also joins in one. Thank you.

When we reflect, we often get to the same point, not because we are looking at the same thing, but because the same thing is looking at us. Many of the troubles we will have in life are a result of our reactions to the world around us. Not to say that there don't exist problems of the world that are beyond a mere change in perspective. Rather, the problems many of us face are not external but internal, and even within external problems we find internal struggles. For all things, give yourself what you can, and most of all, give yourself the moment. When we deprive ourselves of the joy of being ourselves, we desire to be others. When we don't find comfort within the unknown, we will only trot on the paths of other people. In saying this, I stress the idea that neither is wrong, because neither can be right. The one who determines how you live and what you live by is always going to be you. Now whether or not you are aware of this is another inquiry. I wrote all of these in a hope of being able to see myself in a more plain way. Sometimes we have to express ourselves to ourselves in order to find out what we want to express to others. In an effort to find, we often lose many things around it. In our lack of acknowledgement of the self we often try to find it everywhere but where it is.

I would be glad to know this helped someone for I know the way some of these ideas have helped me. There is always more to be discovered both within and without yourself, the importance is to be here for it. As it pertains to novels in the future, trust as long as I am alive they will be underway. Even if not, there are many others who have said and will say the same things, just in a slightly different way. If you aren't here to appreciate what is, then you'll be left appreciating what was. And in your appreciation of what was, you lose what currently is worth appreciation. The objective is to not get lost within your objectives and learn how to be present in anything you are doing, because you are doing it. The problems in the mind tend to be just that, in the mind.

All restriction is born of a mind, so is the same of freedom. You are as trapped as you think you are, and you are as free as you think. For it's not about what contains us, but what we contain within ourselves that truly limits us.

The gold is within

If we base how we feel on what we see

The feeling of the self

Should be a sight to behold

Your life is greater than what you've been told

To see gold is to project the self

For it's your own value that you place in wealth

And I know its emptying to cheat feeling

But think of all the energy wasted

To paths you're kneeled in

They have their time and place

So stay in the present so you don't trace,

The past

Profound Pondering

About the Author

Eyan Bryant is an Author primarily known for his work with the YouTube channel "Profound Pondering". In which he talks frequently about many of the challenges with our mental health, mainly in how we view our own. He is currently a university student and has dedicated himself to learning the main reasons we feel negative about ourselves. He notes that, "The main factor in whether or not you feel comfort in who you are isn't your surroundings, it's your perspective". And in his continual address of the present, he hopes to both come to greater understanding of the world and permit others a chance to do the same.

A word

"When it comes to my mental health journey and work with Profound Pondering, I would say I genuinely started at the age of 14. In the past, I felt as though I was very volatile and very aware of myself in a somewhat negative way. I happened to stumble across a few pieces of literature and videos which would lead me to pursuing a better sense of self through meditation. Through the quarantine period of the Covid-19 pandemic I would spend hours meditating and, in many ways, getting a better feel of who I was, which to me seemed like it took forever. I began to make videos on some of the subjects I would question about and would interview some of my peers at high school which are still up on my channel today. Topics like, does love truly exist? Do soulmates exist? What does it mean to exist? and many questions following ideas of solitude and growth. When it got to a point where I felt like stating my own input, I released a video in a format where I was talking about how the self is created, and my thoughts on change in a general sense. Prior to my video making I would write to great lengths about the topics found in my videos, basing a large portion of what I talked about on those writings. Over the four plus years I have been working with Profound Pondering, it has served as a mental health journey and spiritual guide for me and surprisingly many others who deal with over-thought and negative aspects of their identity. My intention is to continue to move forward with Profound Pondering and allow it along with myself to grow into what I have yet to become."

Noted Works

[1]Nietzsche, Friedrich, et al. *Thus Spoke Zarathustra: The Philosophy Classic*. John Wiley & Sons, Incorporated, 2022.

[2]Shedd, John A. *Salt from My Attic*. Mosher Press, 1928.

[3]Gibran, Kahlil. *The Prophet Kahlil Gibran*. Rupa, 1993.

[4] Nietzsche, Friedrich Wilhelm, and Adrian Del Caro. *Beyond Good and Evil ; on the Genealogy of Morality*. Stanford University Press, 2014.

[5]Jean-Luc Godard, review of *Montparnasse 19*, *Cahiers du Cinéma* 83 (May 1958): n.p. ("Car celui qui saute dans le vide n'a plus de comptes à rendre à ceux qui le regardent.").

[6]Seneca, Lucius Annaeus, and Edward Phillips Barker. *Letters to Lucilius. Translated by E. Phillips Barker*. Clarendon Press, 1932.

[7]Bronte, Anne. The Narrow Way, 1848

[8]"The Dream of Life." Created by Alan Watts, Accessed 2025.

[9]Feynman, Richard, director. *Cargo Cult Science Speech*, 1974, Accessed 2025.

[10]Euripides, and G. S. Kirk. *The Bacchae. A Translation with Commentary by Geoffrey S. Kirk*. Prentice-Hall, 1970.

[11] *Alan Watts, Out of Your Mind: The Nature of Consciousness (Novato, CA: Sounds True, 2004), Lecture 1.*

[12] Inoue, Takehiko. *Vagabond.* Viz Media.

[13] Marcus Aurelius, et al. *Marcus Aurelius: Meditations.* Oxford University Press, 2016.

www.ingramcontent.com/pod-product-compliance
Lightning Source LLC
Chambersburg PA
CBHW060414130626
46555CB00005B/2061

* 9 7 9 8 9 9 9 2 3 9 5 0 1 *